AN INVESTIGATION

INTO THE

CAUSES

OF THE

GREAT FALL IN PRICES

WHICH

TOOK PLACE COINCIDENTLY

WITH THE

DEMONETISATION OF SILVER BY GERMANY.

BY

ARTHUR CRUMP.

1969

GREENWOOD PRESS, PUBLISHERS
NEW YORK

Originally published in 1889
by Longmans, Green, and Co.

First Greenwood Reprinting 1969

PRINTED IN UNITED STATES OF AMERICA

CONTENTS.

INTRODUCTION.

The following brief investigation relates to a subject which has for some time ceased to excite anything like the interest which was felt in it while hopes were still entertained that something might be done in the direction of endeavouring to rehabilitate silver through the joint action of the leading Governments of the world. We have heard of late very few complaints about there being any scarcity of gold, one reason being that business generally is more prosperous, and people are making money in very many cases, instead of losing it or making none, as large numbers did for some years after silver began to fall. We hear nothing, either, about there being any increase in the supply of gold, although we see some of the prices in Mr. Goschen's list, which will be found in an Appendix, rising owing to specific causes, having no relation to the supply of gold, which are plainly set out on p. 197. The reasons for some of the changes downwards in the prices given have been newly procured from the best sources, while the fall in tea is traced from the circulars of an eminent firm in the trade, and disposes effectually of any necessity for seeking for the fall among currency influences. Although, as we have said, keen interest in the question has somewhat subsided, there is no reason on that account to abandon attempts to throw some more light on the real influences which have

A

been at work. With so very complicated a question, it is difficult to classify the subjects for discussion, and, we fear, in this respect we shall be found fault with. The main thing, however, is, to endeavour to produce a result which shall be, as near as possible, a demonstration that prices did not fall owing to a scarcity of gold, but that they did decline owing to other causes, which are definitely assigned as having produced the fall in each case, apart from other and more general causes, which will have affected all to some extent, which will have affected certain groups, and which will have exercised even a still more limited influence. The means and the form are nothing compared with establishing the fact that it is not necessary to attempt to prove that gold, as an element in the problem, exercised no material influence compared with those to whose agency the fall can be shown to have been due. We set out to do this, and we hope we have succeeded.

CHAPTER I.

CONFUSION OF THOUGHT WHICH HAS CHARACTERISED
PREVIOUS ENQUIRIES INTO THE CAUSES OF THE FLUCTUATIONS
IN PRICES.

THE discussions which have been carried on, by means not only of public meetings, but of books, pamphlets and newspapers, ever since the demonetisation of silver by Germany, regarding the influences which many persons believe to have been the direct effect of that act upon the prices of commodities, seem to us to have been characterised by some confusion of thought, which has in our time, as in the past, very much misled the public whenever currency questions have engaged attention. Whether or not we ourselves are justified in stepping into the arena with the object of endeavouring to make somewhat clearer what other people seem to us to have confused by their arguments remains to be seen; but we have been impelled towards this endeavour under the pressure of a belief that a good many people who have formulated their views upon the various causes of the late heavy fall in prices are labouring under delusions, and at the risk of being ourselves on some points wrong, we have decided to make the attempt at a further investigation, beyond a small part* we had previously

---

* *See* in Appendix a letter, entitled, " The Alleged Appreciation in the Value of Gold, and the Fall in the Prices of Commodities," which appeared in the *Economist* of May 19, 1883.

taken, with the object of trying to come nearer to a solution of the problem. We will premise this investigation by going back for light and leading on some deceased renowned authorities—authorities, we believe, as sound, if not sounder than any at present living—for the purpose of clearing the ground and laying down a foundation upon which to build the conclusions we shall endeavour to arrive at.

The fluctuations in prices are well known to have been investigated in the past by persons who were considered by no less an authority than J. S. Mill himself as "the most eminent authorities." We refer, of course, to Messrs. Tooke and Newmarch. Before proceeding to cite the axioms by the light of which those authorities worked, and by whose guidance they arrived at their deductions, we will just refer to a sentence or two of Mill's, in which he speaks of the confusion which has hampered and misled the public at all times when currency questions have occupied the public mind.

Mill remarks in Vol. II. Pol. Econ., p. 10, on Money: " The illustration of these principles, considered in their application to money, must be given in some detail, on account of the confusion which, in minds not scientifically instructed on the subject, envelopes the whole matter; partly from a lingering remnant of the old misleading associations, and partly from the mass of vapoury and baseless speculation with which this, more than any other topic of political economy, has in latter times become surrounded."

Again, at p. 19 he says: " But on a subject so full of complexity as that of currency and prices, it is

necessary to lay the foundation of our theory in a
thorough understanding of the most simple cases,
which we shall always find lying as a ground-work
or substratum under those which arise in practice.
That an increase of the quantity of money raises prices
and a diminution lowers them, is the most elementary
proposition in the theory of currency, and *without it we
should have no key to any of the others.* In a state of
things, however, except *the simple and primitive one
which we have supposed, the proposition only is true,
other things being the same.*" It is necessary to remark
here that this hypothesis, "other things being the same,"
is just the qualification which makes all the difference
when included as an element in the problem. A greater
change had been taking place during several years
previous to the great fall in prices in the "other things"
—*i.e.,* in the circumstances generally affecting the
operation of supply and demand—than had perhaps ever
been witnessed before. We refer, of course, to the
improved means of production, improved machinery,
improved means of communication, to the diminished
purchasing power of certain classes, &c., &c., which is
treated of in detail in the letter to the *Economist* to
which we have referred. J. S. Mill continues: "We
can, however, point out one or two of the cautions with
which the principle must be guarded in attempting
to make use of it for the practical explanation of
phenomena; cautions the more indispensable, as the
doctrine, though a scientific truth, has of late years
been the foundation of a greater mass of false theory and
erroneous interpretation of facts than any other pre-

position relating to interchange. From the time of the resumption of cash payments by the Act of 1819, and especially since the commercial crisis of 1825, *the favourite explanation of every rise or fall of prices has been the currency;* and like most popular theories, the doctrine has been applied with little regard to the conditions necessary for making it correct. For example, it is habitually assumed that whenever there is a greater amount of money in the country, or in existence, *a rise of prices must necessarily follow.** But this is by no means an inevitable consequence. In no commodity is it *the quantity in existence, but the quantity offered for sale, that determines the value.* Whatever may be the quantity of money in the country, only that part of it will affect prices which goes into the market of commodities, and is there actually exchanged against goods. Whatever increases the amount of this portion of the money in the country tends to raise prices. But money hoarded does not act on prices. Money kept in reserve by individuals to meet contingencies which do not occur does not act on prices. The money in the coffers of the Bank, or retained as a reserve by private bankers, does not act on prices until drawn out, nor even then, unless drawn out to be expended in commodities.

" It frequently happens that money to a considerable amount is brought into the country, is there actually invested as capital, and again flows out, without having even once acted upon the markets of commodities, but only upon the markets of securities, or as it is commonly,

---

* The italics are ours.

though improperly, called, the money market. Let us return to the case already put for illustration, that of a foreigner landing in the country with a treasure. We supposed him to employ his treasure in the purchase of goods for his own use, or in setting up a manufactory and employing labourers; and in either case he would, *cæteris paribus*, raise prices. But instead of doing either of these things, he might very probably prefer to invest his fortune at interest, which we shall suppose him to do in the most obvious way—by becoming a competitor for a portion of the stock, Exchequer bills, railway debentures, mercantile bills, mortgages, &c., which are at all times in the hands of the public. By doing this he would raise the prices of those different securities, or, in other words, would lower the rate of interest; and since this would disturb the relation previously existing between the rate of interest on capital in the country itself and that in foreign countries, it would probably induce some of those who had floating capital seeking employment to send it abroad for foreign investment, rather than buy securities at home at the advanced price. As much money might thus go out as had previously come in, while the prices of commodities would have shown no trace of its temporary presence. This is a case highly deserving of attention; and it is a fact now beginning to be recognised, that the passage of the precious metals from country to country is determined much more than was formerly supposed by the state of the loan market in different countries, and much less by the state of prices."

Writing in the *Economist* of April, 1845, on the

subject of currency and banking, Mr. John Wilson remarked: "This confusion is apparent in most of the discussions and writings of that time, and in a great majority of all that have appeared since, and in no place in a more remarkable degree than in the speeches with which Sir Robert Peel introduced and supported his new Bank Bill last year."

Having shown how easily even writers of repute have fallen into error in treating these complicated questions, we must endeavour to proceed warily a step at a time, and to avoid as much as possible that dangerous practice of prematurely deviating into side issues. It is here that so many writers on these subjects are lured into the jungle of difficulties, in which they only further entangle themselves the more they struggle to get out.

These few citations sufficiently establish the fact that there has been much confusion in the past among some of those who have endeavoured to explain the causes of the fluctuations in prices, and in order to avoid falling into the same errors, we cannot do better than collect from the writings of the best authorities the statements of fact by the light of which they arrived at what the best subsequent authorities accept as sound deductions. Now, the point which seems to call for attention on the threshold of our investigation is, that the opinions held by so many persons in our day as to the cause of the fall in prices which took place coincidently with the heavy depreciation of silver consequent on its demonetisation by Germany, appear to have been formed by the light of principles which have been more or less undermined, and thus rendered inoperative as maxims, such as that "an increase in the quantity of money raises prices and a diminution lowers them," which, as Mill remarks, is ONLY true in a simple and primitive state, *other things being the same.*

One of the great difficulties which has troubled investigators in connection with this question is that of proving to what extent the volume of actively circulating currency has actually increased or diminished, and to what extent changes in prices can be ascribed to those fluctuations. When prices have moved either way, it has been assumed that the quantity of metal currency has increased or diminished to an extent sufficiently to account for the movement in prices; but no attempt to demonstrate such a proposition by verified data has ever been made, so far as we know. At best it has only been an inference, and we are of opinion that it can only be an inference, owing to the intangible nature of the data necessary, on the currency side, to enable a complete demonstration to be arrived at. The demonstration on the other side, by means of the verifiable data outside currency influences, can be rendered sufficiently complete to justify the investigator in coming to the conclusion that, although currency influences exercised some influence in the present case, it was practically immaterial. This is our view, in fact, of the lines upon which an investigation should be undertaken, and upon which we think it can be satisfactorily carried through. We are further of opinion that what has come to light since this matter first came up for discussion, now already some years ago, satisfactorily establishes the fact that an investigation on such lines will yield the desired solution, while no other can. The object of this investigation is to show that there was no scarcity of gold, but rather the contrary, and further to demonstrate by positive evidence that prices fell owing to causes outside currency influences.

Let us now get a foothold first of all upon a piece of concrete ground, where we can take our stand, and only leave it when we have laid a bit more of concrete foundation to which we can safely pass.

First of all, then, the starting-point is the *standard of value.* A medium of exchange and a standard of value are created but for one object, and that is the facilitation of the exchange of commodities. They are instruments to that end, and nothing more. All are agreed on that point, and therefore we can at once proceed to the proposition, equally impossible to refute, viz., that efforts have always been made to keep in circulation the *smallest* quantity of currency consistently with the requirements of business. Here, then, we have two concrete stepping-stones which lead up to the conclusions we are making for, the objects striven for in practice being—

1. Facilitation of exchange ;
2. At the least cost.

Let us examine the first, just to see, in passing, how the propositions of the bi-metallists are compatible with the automatic working of the facilitation of exchange upon the most economical principles. That, of course, is an indispensable element in every sound system of currency. All engaged in commerce and banking have been struggling from the first to diminish the friction involved in the exchange of commodities, and why? because friction means (1) expense, (2) delay. The very instincts of traders would therefore guide them in the direction of removing as fast as they could from their path everything existing in the shape of cumbersome currency.

We do not need to show how these two objects have ceaselessly been striven for in the past by the united efforts of all to save their time and money: we will then merely take for granted that that proposition is proved, and bring forward the latest evidence in further support of it which has been placed before the public, and which we have taken from the *St. James's Gazette*, as there transplanted from the *Economist*.

ECONOMIES IN THE USE OF COIN.

The second report of the Gold and Silver Commission issued this week contains some interesting information with regard to the economies in the use of coin that have been effected in England during recent years. The most important evidence on this branch of the subject was that given by Mr. Bertram W. Currie. After reminding the Commission that between 1873 and 1886 the number of bank branches in England and Wales increased from 1,100 to 1,755, he went on to show, from the experience of the bank with which he himself is connected—Glyn, Mills and Co.—what the effect of this extension of banking facilities has been. Comparing three days in 1880 with three days in 1887, he said:—

In 1880 the total number of cheques drawn on country banks for which Glyn's acted as agents was in three selected days 19,950, and the number of them under 1*l.* was 462, or 2¼ per cent. of the whole. In 1887 the total number of cheques in the three corresponding days was 35,090, against 19,950, and 1,481 of these were under 1*l.*, 4 per cent. of the whole, so that in these seven years the percentage of cheques under 1*l.* has increased from 2¼ per cent. to 4 per cent., and the total has increased from 19,950 to 35,090. Then over 1*l.* and under 5*l.* in the first period, 1880, there were 5,229 cheques in three days, or 26 per cent. of the whole; and in the second period, 1887, there were 11,682, or 32 per cent., so that the ratio of increase is largest in the small denomination, and that, I think, is a strong argument in favour of what I have said; and if there was any scarcity of gold, substitutes would be found which would remove any inconvenience, or would obviate the evil of any such scarcity.

And dealing separately with suburban cheques, he stated that whereas in 1880 Glyn's dealt with 620 of such cheques daily, of which ninety-three were between £5 and £10, and 215 under £5, in 1887 they dealt with 1,250 cheques daily, of which 245 were between £5 and £10, and 515 under £5. It is thus evident that the multiplication of branch banks has greatly economised the use of gold. As Mr. Currie put it, small traders, who previously had no banking account, and were consequently compelled each to keep a certain amount of gold in their shops, have now opened accounts, and the cash they previously held has been liberated. Evidence of a somewhat similar character was given by Mr. William Fowler, who submitted the following statement of the country clearing of Messrs. Barclay for the months of November, 1882 to 1886 :—

November.	Number of Cheques.	Total Amount.	Average per Cheque.
1886	45,310	£1,131,300	£24·9
1885	42,370	1,056,200	29·9
1884	41,750	1,192,900	28·5
1883	40,710	1,194,900	28·8
1882	38,670	1,163,400	30·1

Here, as the *Economist* observes, we have a considerable increase in the number of cheques accompanied by a still greater proportionate decrease in the average amount for which the cheques were drawn; and the teaching from the figures is, that in the retail business of the country cheques are taking the place of coin. Another economy to which Mr. Currie directed attention is the displacement of coin by postal notes.

Take, he says, the postal orders, which were only established in 1881-82. The postal orders in 1881-82 were in number four and a-half millions, and in amount £2,000,000 sterling; in 1885-86 they were in number twenty-five and three-quarter millions, and in amount £10,750,000 sterling. During the same period postal money-orders, which to a certain extent may be said to compete with them, remained nearly stationary—that is to say, the amount in the first period was £23,250,000, and in the second period £22,000,000. Therefore it could not be said that the postal orders had displaced the money orders. Well, then, I have taken the following from our own experience: at Glyn's bank, 2,000 postal orders are dealt with daily now, as against 500 postal orders six years ago.

Again, while in various ways we have been contriving to make a little gold do the work which previously it took much gold to accomplish, we are keeping a considerable stock of the metal lying idle.

We thus, in brief, demonstrate that at all times and in all circumstances the great object has always been to do with the currency as with the working of a railway train, to bring friction down to the minimum, and to grease the wheels at the least expense. It is all a question of cost in both cases. If there is much trade there will be more money, or its representative, circulating. *The money can never increase first*, while Governments continue to coin money in response to the increasing requirements of trade. Its increase follows that of the trade. Why? Because more money circulating means more money *spent* in buying the metal, and more money *spent* in coining and maintaining it in circulation. If trade decreases money goes out of circulation, and is melted down and either hoarded or sold, just as the railway carriages are disposed of where the traffic has so fallen off as not to require them any longer.

What, then, is the *rationale* of this demonstrated proposition? Simply, that now, as at all other times, if commodities were not exchangeable with the utmost facility consistently with the development of other parts of the machinery of commerce and banking and at the least cost which the ingenuity of man has been so far able to devise, the community would cry out, as they have always cried out before, until such amendments were introduced as the sense of the sound-thinking portion of the community demanded. To this some will say, " Some of them are crying out!" We reply, " Who are they? Do they constitute one per mille, and is there one sound economist among them ? "

The position, then, that we arrive at, so far, is this, that the currency is an automatic machine, working under similar influences to those which govern prices generally, with this important exception, that when the supply of precious metal exceeds the demand a much longer time is required to consume the surplus than in the case of any other commodity.

What is the great principle that governs prices? *Supply and demand.* Another way of putting this is the following, which we may repeat with advantage, viz. : — It is not the quantity of a commodity in existence that determines the value, but it is *the quantity offered for sale.*

If the owners of the Newcastle coal fields were to find out that it would be in their interests to undersell all other sellers of coal, as the German Government undersold all other sellers of silver, would it be thought sensible of other coal mine owners to rush about Europe, and try to persuade people who were not interested in maintaining the price of coal to combine for that purpose? Wherein consists the difference between the silver and the coal? They are both commodities, and are governed, as regards their value, by the same laws, silver not being entitled in the smallest degree to be treated differently from coal.

To reinstate silver on the lines demanded by the bi-metallists would be as sensible a proceeding as endeavouring to compete with the railways by reviving the old stage coaches. This becomes at once apparent when one single fact is brought forward, which we believe we do no injustice in saying that not many people include it in their calculations. It is this, that a large and increasing quantity of circulating coin, which was formerly needed in a rougher state of our currency machinery, is now collected in the banks, and unless the existing confidence between individuals and nations becomes destroyed by revolutions or wars, has been as good as again consigned to the bowels of the earth from which it was extracted.

The great bulk of the gold held by the great European national banks is never moved, and is never likely to be, unless in circumstances such as we have mentioned. While the greatest powers stand together politically for mutual protection, as they stand now, the confidence between man and man and between nation and nation, which has relieved the precious metals of the duties imposed upon them in a state of civilisation when a man could not get an umbrella without having the sovereign in his hand to pay for it, will be maintained, and the medium of exchange will become more and more a promise to pay on the thinnest piece of paper that can be manufactured consistently with sufficient strength. Thus we are, and have been for a long time past, in the presence of a movement which is entirely opposed to any idea of extending or enlarging the metallic machinery of the currency. The changes that are taking place are in an opposite direction, and will, there is every reason to believe, so continue.

CHAPTER II.

1. Prices are the expression in coin of the realm of the relative worth of commodities.

2. The appreciation or depreciation of the value in commodities of these coins can only be caused by the decrease or increase respectively of the amount of those coins in circulation, and the change is generally a very slow one. For example: if more coins are drawn into active circulation, prices which have risen through the exercise of greater purchasing power will remain higher if the necessity of a larger active circulation is maintained.

3. Therefore, to produce any effect upon prices at all one way or the other, it is not sufficient that there be a greater or less production of the metals used, but that there be first an increase of purchasing power, and that that increase operate sensibly upon the mass of coined money not only in one country, but in all countries using those metals. This was proved by the action of Germany in demonetising her silver. High prices are a distinct disadvantage, because a greater proportion of capital must be kept employed to circulate commodities. Prices having fallen, less money is required to circulate commodities.

The rise or fall in prices should be in proportion to that which the increase in the gold bears to that previously in circulation. Do those who attribute the fall in prices to an appreciation of gold maintain that a proportion of the amount in circulation equal to the proportionate fall in prices had disappeared from the metal circulation? Because it is only by removing it from the active circulation, as we have said, that such an effect upon prices as a whole could be produced. If our investigation shows anything, it demonstrates that gold was drawn from the hoards into active circulation, and that the facts thus show that an opposite effect would have been produced but for the circumstance that the withdrawal of silver left a void in the necessary volume of the German circulating medium; and secondly, that less coined money was required in proportion to the fall in prices. The domestic circulation of gold has probably increased, while the international circulation of bullion has unquestionably largely decreased.

Mill says, in his "Political Economy," Vol. II., p. 19: "When credit comes into play as a means of purchasing, distinct from money in hand. . . . *The connection between prices and the amount of the circulating medium is much less direct and intimate.*" And again at p. 22: "An increase in the circulating medium conformable in extent and duration to the temporary stress of business does not raise prices, but merely prevents a fall." The converse of this proposition would be, that a decrease in the circulating medium "conformable in extent and duration" to the decline in the activity of trade does not cause a fall in prices, but merely prevents a rise.

As a result of the stagnation of trade there is a gradual consumption of surplus commodities, the declining prices not encouraging producers to burden themselves with stocks. A contraction of the volume of purchasing power causes food, &c., to become cheaper through economised consumption, while there will be a better yield as the result of more efficient individual labour.

A contraction of credit and consequent fall in prices draws gold into the country. Gold, however, is oftener attracted by a fall in securities, which is the result of a rise in the rate of interest, while the prices of commodities are not affected.

The effect upon prices of the fluctuations in the market value of money through the expansion and contraction of credit is quite a different thing from the effect upon prices caused by an increase in the volume of money circulating, which is the result of a demand for it to facilitate the exchange of a greater quantity of commodities.

Mill says, Vol. II. " Political Economy," p. 39 : " In a state of commerce in which much credit is habitually given, general prices at any moment depend much more upon the state of credit than upon the quantity of money."

Political economists have agreed that the *average* prices of commodities, taken as a whole, are determined by the cost of producing the precious metals. An ounce of gold ought to exchange for as much of other commodities as require for their production the same expenditure of labour and capital. But this is one of those axioms whose force, like others we have referred to, diminishes under the influence of changing circumstances. The "other things" (not) "remaining the same" to which Mill referred alter the position materially. For instance, at the present time a silver shilling of the realm buys more than a piece of the same weight uncoined. This is proved by the fact that the Government has made large gains by its coinage of silver since the price fell. The above axiom would only hold good so long as the gold miner could take his gold to the mint and get it coined at will. The current value of silver coins would have sunk lower had the mints been open for free coinage. There are consequently two different values for both metals. The gold in circulation as coin will buy much more than if all the gold in existence were coined and put in circulation. This proves that gold may exist largely in excess of currency or mercantile requirements, and yet exercise no effect whatever upon prices. The German, United States, Italian and other requirements were taken from the uncoined excess, and therefore did not directly affect prices.

An article which, owing to changed circumstances, can be produced more cheaply than before, or whose value has fallen owing to its diminished utility, which is always an element in value, will buy less gold, and therefore *in relation to that particular* article gold may be said to have appreciated. Most of the prices have thus fallen, not owing, as some allege, to the appreciation of

gold, but owing to circumstances affecting their individual value either as regards cost of production or
diminished demand or utility.

It should be remembered that the prices of
commodities may deviate very widely from that which
is their cost of production; that the extent to which an
individual can influence prices is just so much as the
extent of the purchasing power which he is able to
exercise; and, further, that speculative purchases may
considerably raise some prices, while others are un-
affected. Mere book credit purchases have the same
effect when they are made as if actual money passed;
and, again, it should never be forgotten, that after
a period of great inflation prices fall often as much
below their normal level as they were previously
forced above, through the forced sales of traders
who cannot obtain the accommodation they require,
owing to a want of confidence arising out of the
commercial revulsion. Such fall need not be due
to anything affecting money, *but owing to a contraction
of credit.*

There is no doubt that silver has fallen in value,
owing to its diminished utility, which is a direct
consequence of its production having so exceeded
requirements as to render it less fitted to perform
the functions of a standard of value than before, and
some people argue that gold must have risen in value in
proportion, owing to its having been absorbed to fill the
vacuum. Let us examine this. Very little attention
seems to have been directed to the question of hoards
in this discussion, which is a point bearing very

materially upon the solution of this problem. The
supply of gold that was purchased for coinage purposes
by Germany and other countries would, it stands to
reason, be first taken from the most available sources,
the circulating currency being always the last to be
touched, for obvious reasons. Unless the actual circulating currency is trenched upon, thus operating by
degrees over the whole area of currencies, there can be
no permanent general fall in prices, even from their
normal average level. It is well known that
Mr. Goschen's prices were very much above the normal
level.

We have said that Mr. Goschen's figures, upon
which he based his deductions that the fall in
prices was due to a scarcity of gold, were greatly
inflated. In proof of that contention we quote a
statement of Mr. Mundella from the *Times*, reported
in the debate on the depression of trade on 31st
October, 1884 :

"Mr. Mundella said that the hon. gentleman had
compared the periods between the years 1869 and 1873,
and the years 1879 and 1883. But that period com-
prised those tremendous years of inflation when steel
rails, now selling at £5 a ton, were selling at £20 a ton,
and when iron was three times its present price. It
also included the period of the Franco-German War,
when, in fact, the whole manufacture of Europe was
thrown upon this country; and therefore it was hardly
fair to compare those two periods. Within the period
1879-83 every kind of manufacture was lower than it
had ever been in the memory of man. In the cotton

trade the quantity of raw material imported in 1878 was 1,176,500 lbs.; in 1879, 1,173,326 lbs.; in 1882, 1,461,900 lbs.; and in 1883, 1,510,600 lbs. As to the exports, of course the price of shirtings and such articles depended on the price of the raw cotton at Liverpool; and in 1878, the quantity of cotton piece-goods exported was 3,618,665 yards; in 1882, 4,349,391 yards; and in 1883, 4,538,889 yards; so that regularly in that department of industry there had been a large increase in the exports. Then there was an enormous increase in the annual amount of the deposits in the Post Office and trustees' banks. In 1878 the amount was £19,344,000; in 1879, £19,547,000; in 1882 it rose to £23,354,000; and in 1883 to £24,123,000, or an increase of nearly 20 per cent. Then, again, what were the facts with regard to the income tax? In 1879 the returns under Schedules A, B, C, D and E amounted to £578,000,000, and in 1882 to £601,000,000. Now, he would give the other side of the picture, and give some account of France, which was a protective country, and had been for some time carefully nursing her trade. During the eight months ending August 31, 1882, 1883, and 1884, the value of the principal manufactured articles exported from France was £48,895,000, £45,836,000, and £41,493,000 respectively; and the total exports, including agricultural produce, were in 1882, £92,217,000; in 1883, £87,611,000; and in 1884, £81,617,000. Let them look at the contrast of the two countries, and see which system was producing the better results for its people. The hon. member had said that the nation had been fed upon promises for the last 40 years. All he could say was, that anything more terrible than the general suffering of the population 40 years ago it was impossible to describe. When he was a youth it was for the handloom weavers a life of chronic starvation; they never had enough to eat, and the condition of the artisans in the midland counties was one of terrible and constant suffering. This did not begin to amend until the Corn Laws were repealed."

The gold introduced into the German monetary system was not abstracted from the circulation of other countries, but was taken from hoards, or from the reserves of bankers; consequently, there was, in fact, no decrease in the gold currencies of some countries in order to provide what Germany required. As far as the operations of Germany were concerned, the gold put by them into circulation to replace that of the silver which they sold was as good as abstracted from the bowels of the earth. Consequently, there could be no real appreciation in the value of the metal in relation to commodities as a whole, but, if anything, a depreciation, as a result of the quantity in circulation being greater than before. In a sense, it can be said that gold has appreciated because you can buy more for a sovereign than you could before the fall in prices; but we are of opinion that it cannot be maintained with strict scientific accuracy that the circulating medium can be said to have risen in value because some other commodities have depreciated. We shall have something more to say on this subject farther on.

When Germany decided upon introducing a gold currency, there was no disturbance of the equation of international demand for commodities arising directly from that introduction. The exchange was not in her favour to the extent of compelling other countries to export gold to Germany, in order to adjust any adverse trade balance. It is seen, therefore, that the gold was imported as a commodity on the same basis as if it had been wool, cotton, or tea; and that the movement was powerless to affect directly prices which, as far as currency influences are concerned, can only be affected over long periods by gradual changes in the whole volume circulating.

If it can be proved, then, to demonstration, which we believe it can, that the movements of bullion do not affect prices as a whole until that movement either adds to or subtracts from the gold in actual circulation as coin, the increase even then being the effect and not the cause, we seem to arrive at a proof that general prices could not have been affected by the demonetisation of silver by Germany in any other way than as a result of the fall in the price of the commodity silver, and as a result of the indirect loss thereby sustained by a multitude of interests which were bound up in the retention of the value of silver at the price from which it fell. That there was a multitude of interests sorely affected by that fall in the value of silver is attested by the complaints of bimetallists, nearly all of whom are directly interested in rehabilitating silver, which have been heard ever since, and by the destruction wrought among the numbers of corporate bodies and individuals whose property in the East has fallen in value *pari passu* with that of silver. The stimulus given to the export of Eastern produce to Europe by the fall in the Eastern exchanges is matter of common notoriety, and would of itself account for a large part of the fall in Mincing Lane prices. The fall which took place was, there can be no doubt, very largely the result of speculation for the fall among those who were clever enough to see what must be the result of the decline in the Eastern exchanges. But we have to reckon beyond this with the decline in the prices of European manufactured articles which have been exported to pay for these increased imports of Eastern produce. With all the complaints of the depression of trade, we know that the volume of both imports and exports has remained as great as before, if not larger, which proves that to call it depression of trade is a misnomer. It is really a depression of profits, owing to the decline in values, aggravated by increased competition, both among manufacturers and producers of the raw material.

Mr. Tooke said, in 1832, before the Commons Committee on the Bank Charter question: " In point of fact and historically, as far as my researches have gone, in every signal instance of a rise or fall of prices, the rise or fall *has preceded*, and therefore could not be *the effect of*, an enlargement or contraction of the bank circulation."

Mr. Fullerton also said at the same time, " That bank issues, since they cannot be increased in amount unless there be an increased demand, cannot possibly raise prices." Mr. J. S. Mill accepts this as incontrovertible.

The demand of a Government for gold to establish a gold standard is a very different thing from an increasing demand for more currency in response to an increase in the trade of a country, which gives rise to a greater and more active interchange of commodities. Such increase and greater activity respectively, being due to the exercise of more extended purchasing power, would first cause a rise in prices, which would be followed by a natural expansion of the circulating medium.

Regarding the vast accumulations of treasure known to exist in France so long ago as when Mr. Fullerton wrote his treatise* on the subject of currencies, he then said: "Of this vast treasure (estimated to amount to £120,000,000 sterling) there is every reason to presume that a very large proportion, probably much the greater part, is absorbed in the hoards. . . . That the quantity of specie accumulated in these innumerable depôts not only in France, but all over the Continent, where banking institutions are still either entirely wanting or very imperfectly organised, is not merely immense in itself, but admits of being largely drawn upon, and transferred even in vast masses from one country to another with *very little, if any, effect on prices*, or other material derangements, we have had some remarkable proofs": among others, "the signal success which attended the simultaneous efforts of some of the principal European Powers (Russia, Austria, Prussia, Sweden and Denmark) to replenish their treasuries, and to replace

* Fullerton on the "Regulation of Currencies."

with coin a considerable portion of the depreciated paper which the necessities of the war had forced upon them, and this at the very time when the available stock of the precious metals over the world had been reduced by the exertions of England to recover her metallic currency. . . . There can be no doubt that these combined operations were on a scale of very extraordinary magnitude, that they were accomplished without any sensible injury to commerce or public prosperity, or any other effect than some temporary derangement of the exchanges, and that the private hoards of treasure accumulated throughout Europe during the war must have been the principal source from which all this gold and silver was collected. And no person, I think, can fairly contemplate the vast superflux of metallic wealth thus proved to be at all times in existence, and, though in a dormant and inert state, always ready to spring into activity on the first indication of a sufficiently intense demand, without feeling themselves compelled to admit the possibility of the mines being even shut up for years together, and the production of the metals altogether suspended, *while there might be scarcely a perceptible alteration in the exchangeable value of the metal.*" This evidence, from a very competent authority, seems to lessen very much the force of Mr. Goschen's argument that the £200,000,000, supposing such a sum were taken clean out of existing active circulating currencies, which it was not, absorbed ten years' supply, estimated at a yearly average of £20,000,000.

Further referring to the currency doctrine and its

advocates, Mr. Fullerton wrote: "One might imagine that they supposed the gold which is drained off for exportation from a country using a currency exclusively metallic to be collected by dribblets at the fairs and markets, or from the tills of the grocers and mercers. They never even allude to the existence of such a thing as a great hoard of the metals, though upon the action of the hoards depends the whole economy of international payments between specie-circulating communities, *while any operation of the money collected in hoards upon prices* must, even according to the currency hypothesis, *be wholly impossible.*"

From Fullerton's "Political Economy" we find the following quoted in J. S. Mill's "Political Economy," Vol. II., p. 223: "To come to the present time (1844), the balance of payments with nearly all Europe has for about four years past been in favour of this country, and gold has been pouring in, till the influx amounts to the unheard-of sum of about fourteen millions sterling. Yet in all this time has anyone heard a complaint of any serious suffering inflicted on the people of the Continent? *Have prices there been greatly depressed beyond their range in this country?* Have wages fallen, or have merchants been extensively ruined by the universal depreciation of their stock? There has occurred nothing of the kind. The tenor of commercial and monetary affairs has been everywhere even and tranquil; and in France more particularly, an improving revenue and extended commerce bear testimony to the continued progress of internal prosperity."

What it is all-important should be kept in mind is, that prices are not only not depressed or raised in these times appreciably by additions to or abstractions from the circulating currency, but that if they were, the operation of cause and effect would be in an inverse order to that which is generally believed.

Here we must introduce a leading axiom, which must be firmly grasped before it is possible to understand the real causes by which prices are influenced, and it is this:—" It is the quantity of money constituting the revenues of the different orders of the State, under the head of rents, profits, salaries, and wages, destined for current expenditure, according to the wants and habits of the several classes, *that alone forms the limiting principle of the aggregate of money prices*— the only prices that can properly come under the designation of *general prices*. As the cost of production is the limiting principle of supply, so the aggregate of money incomes devoted to expenditure for consumption is the limiting principle of demand for commodities."* It is most important to keep a clear view of the application of those two principles, as Mr. Tooke felt himself, and he leaves a record in his book of his impressions on that particular point on the same page from which we have taken the foregoing extract, as follows:—" A view to those simple and constantly operative principles, instead of the doctrine of the effects of expansions and contractions of the quantity of paper-money issued by the

---

* Tooke's " History of Prices," p. 276.

Bank, will serve to throw a steady light upon the circumstances determining the general state of trade and of prices."

How little the actual fluctuations in the quantity of currency affected prices, even so long ago as 1840, when Mr. Tooke wrote his book, and how much was due to other causes, is seen from what he wrote when then investigating this question. He says: "The *rationale* of the matter, as appears to me, is this: Prices are the result of a certain ratio between the quantity of money entering into the markets for commodities and the quantity of commodities offering for sale on the other; but the money, or *that which performs the office of money*, that enters into the produce or wholesale markets consists in a very small—I believe an infinitely small—proportion of bank notes. Nine-tenths, or more probably, ninety-nine hundredths, of the purchases and sales of the wholesale markets are transacted through the medium of book debts, or simple credit, and cheques on bankers. It is the balances only of these transactions that require the intervention of bank notes; and it depends partly on the proportion of buyers and sellers who keep accounts with the same banker whether any beyond the smallest possible amount of bank notes is employed for the final adjustment of the largest wholesale transactions in the markets for commodities." If *the proportion* of the money with which commodities were purchased in 1840 was "infinitely small," how much smaller will it be now, with the increase in the number of banks, the greater confidence and intelligence which exists among all trading classes, to say nothing of the purchases and sales that are effected by means of the telegraph, in many different forms, which act upon prices just as if solid gold were the purchasing power.

Mill cites almost, if not quite, a parallel case of a movement of gold as having taken place about the year 1844. It was not so large as that which followed the demonetisation of silver by Germany, supposing always that the estimate given is correct; but then we must remember that a good deal of the gold taken from England for coinage purposes quitted that country as soon as it was put in circulation, causing a great outcry among the Berlin financiers, who did not seem to have allowed for such a contingency. What was the result? Before effective measures could be taken to prevent it draining away across the frontier into France, much of the new coinage had entirely disappeared, and the work had to be done over again, fresh supplies being purchased. It is easy to understand, under these circumstances, that the amount of gold apparently absorbed for German coinage purposes was greatly in excess of what actually entered permanently into the currency of that country. Indeed, it is doubtful if the greater part of it is not at this moment either in the German military chest or in the vaults of the Imperial Bank, which would mean that the hoards let loose by the Franco-German War, and drawn upon afterwards, have returned to their hiding-places, without, as the authorities we have cited testify regarding previous movements, having directly exercised any material effect upon prices at all.

The only material fall in prices which takes place

in these times as a consequence of large bullion movements is the fall in securities which takes place in response to a rise in the rate of interest. Foreigners step in and buy the securities, and the adverse balance is thus adjusted without the currency being affected in the remotest degree.

The foregoing pages contain, we think, ample evidence from the best authorities against the theory that the rapid fall in prices experienced on the occasion under review has been due any more to an alteration in the volume of active currency than was at any previous period the cause of a fall. We have shown that the best authorities agree that an alteration in the volume of the currency is always the effect and not the cause of a general change in prices upwards or downwards. Investigations having proved that it is so, the demonstration must hold good until somebody can upset the evidence on which it is founded. J. S. Mill is not the sort of man to accept the evidence of Tooke, Fullerton, and others, if he were not satisfied that it was correct. If Mr. Goschen, and those who think with him, adhere to their view, they are bound to upset the evidence which seems to us to overthrow their argument, or acknowledge that they are in the wrong.

So far, therefore, it appears that the best deceased authorities are agreed that for general prices to be either raised or lowered there must be a sensible addition to or subtraction from the whole stock of metals in active circulation in all countries, and that such addition to or subtraction from the stock is not the *cause* of a rise or a fall in prices, but is in all cases the consequence. Additions to or subtractions from the currencies of the world are, in other words, due, on the one hand, to a demand for more currency, either to satisfy the requirements of a larger number of inhabitants and to exchange commodities which have risen to higher prices, or to assist in distributing a larger quantity of commodities; and, on the other hand, subtractions are due to either a shrinkage of inhabitants, which would naturally throw the circulating medium, like any other agency, out of employment to some extent, to a decline in prices, or to a diminution in the quantity of commodities to be distributed. It may be said, *à propos* of these remarks, that we have admitted that when the metals could be forced through the mints prices were raised by an increase in the volume of the currency. The quantity of coined money being thus increased would, of course, gradually cause a rise in prices; but the supply of silver from the mines has never until of late years been so excessive as to threaten to exercise a palpably injurious influence upon the creditor class of the community, and when it did, the mints were closed to private coiners. At previous periods a rise in prices from that cause has, as we have particularly pointed out in the letter to the *Economist* in the Appendix, been so very slow as to be scarcely perceptible to a generation. What we are now dealing with is a fall of prices which was so rapid as in itself to carry the proof with it that it was due to causes quite apart from any change in the volume of the precious metals in active circulation.

Up to this point we have been dealing chiefly with

negative evidence, with the object of demonstrating, as we venture to think, that the reasons adduced for asserting that the fall in prices after the Franco-German War had no material relation to a change in the purchasing power of gold as the consequence of an alleged scarcity of that metal, and that, in fact, there has been no material change in that purchasing power *which is due to a scarcity of that metal;* but that its so-called appreciation in relation to some commodities is due simply to those commodities having fallen in price, owing to the supply of them having, for various reasons, exceeded the demand, or to their relative value having declined through diminished utility. This, be it observed, is a proposition differing essentially from that of Mr. Goschen and endorsed by Mr. Giffen, and if it can be made out, by showing with positive evidence, that the fall in certain commodities was due entirely to causes affecting those commodities individually, the premises, and consequently the deductions, of those gentlemen will, we venture to think, be proved to be unsound.

Mr. McCulloch, we shall show further on, was of opinion that silver could rise or fall in price "without its being occasioned by a corresponding fall or rise in gold."

The following extract from Mill touches upon the Californian gold discoveries, which many thought at the time, and apparently still think, was the direct cause of the rise in prices that took place in many articles, through the increase in the active gold currency :

" The discovery of that gold gave rise to what was equivalent to a new industry while it lasted. The gold came to Europe and was sold, the English manufactures of all kinds being returned to the miners, who founded colonies where they were working. The result of the rise in prices thus occasioned increased the currency requirements, and for the time there is no doubt much of that gold was maintained in active circulation, sustaining prices while the greater and more widespread purchasing power was exercised."

It is true that when the equation of international demand is unable to establish itself and the exchanges are adverse, gold flows out until the contraction of credit as a consequence of a rise in the rate of interest has brought the inflated prices either of securities or of some commodities we may have to sell down to a point that will induce the foreigner to buy, and thus adjust the balance; but such a movement exercises no sensible effect upon the great volume of a nation's active currency, so as to influence the normal level of general prices. Over-trading is thus corrected; but in the case under review there was no contraction of the circulation, or any adverse movement in the exchanges. The gold required was taken either from reserves or hoards, so as to avoid even affecting the money market; so that no material effect on prices such as we have seen could result directly from those operations.

Mr. Wilson, the founder of the *Economist*, in writing upon the influences which are exercised by the various operations connected with the trade of the country, remarks as follows: "With a purely metallic currency, in all cases the circulation would be acted upon last, and as an indirect consequence of other causes, but in the case of an import and an export of bullion, it would only be in extreme cases that the circulation would be acted upon at all; for in case of an adverse exchange, which only went so far as to reduce the reserve of coin in the Bank to the proper proportion to the deposits, and there stopped, a considerable export of bullion might take place without any derangement of business, or *any sensible contraction of the circulation*." This was exactly what took place during the operation of Germany's change of standard. The first effect of an import or export of gold to correct the exchanges is always produced exclusively on the bullion reserve of the Bank of England. That is the first to be touched and the circulation last. It may be urged in reply to this, that as the gold leaves the Bank for export the note circulation is contracted. That is true; but even then there is simply a temporary contraction of credit. The movement in these times never goes so far as to cause a material decline in general prices. It is well known that all the countries which are spoken of as having absorbed these £200,000,000 of gold took it designedly, so as to disturb the money markets and trade as little as possible. There was practically no influence exercised on the foreign exchanges by these operations, and consequently the prices even of securities which are the first to suffer as soon as bullion begins to move on any scale were not disturbed, much less the prices of commodities.

If our premises so far are sound, viz., that more

coined money can only be drawn into circulation by an increase of purchasing power or an extension of credit, which, if used, is the same thing, and that prices will remain higher while the increased demand for commodities is maintained, and with it the increased volume of currency, we can demonstrate by converse reasoning that if gold were not required to be drawn from the hoards, what was needed must have been liberated from active circulation by the decline in prices. In brief, the exercise of more purchasing power means more active circulation, and *vice versâ*. Consequently, we seem to be justified in concluding that there could be no resulting scarcity of gold, but exactly the opposite.

CHAPTER III.

SOME OF THE PRINCIPAL CAUSES OF THE DECLINE IN PRICES
WHICH ARE THE SUBJECT OF THIS INVESTIGATION.

A FALL in profits lowers to some extent the cost of
things which are manufactured by machinery.

The significance of this axiom becomes apparent
when considered in connection with the revolution in
production generally which has been developing in this
and other countries for years past. All who follow at
all the progress of manufacturing industry must be
aware that there has been an enormous development
of late years in the capacity both of this and other
countries to turn out articles by machinery which were
previously made by hand-looms and the like. Even
boots and shoes in our day are made by machinery.
This country, as is equally well known, for a long time
enjoyed practically a monopoly in the manufacture of
large machinery, for instance; but in recent years other
countries have worked up level with most of our manufacturers, and whereas formerly it was hardly necessary
for our manufacturers to heed the feeble efforts of other
nations to manufacture for themselves, now not a few of
our people are apprehensive on the score of whether even
they can hold their own in respect of some articles in
which our foreign rivals possess some indigenous or
other advantage over us. From the newspapers we

continue almost daily to realise the fact that our Continental competitors, particularly the Germans, are meeting us in distant markets with a formidable rivalry, which means not only that they can manufacture more goods than their own people can consume, but that they possess surplus energy and resources, which enable them to divert to their own country a portion of the stream of profits which formerly flowed to these islands. These facts are so patent, that it is unnecessary to produce statistics in support of them. They, however, throw a searching light upon the gradual transformation which has been making such perceptible progress in the direction of undermining that preponderance which has hitherto characterised the manufacturing industry of this country.

Now the first thing that happens when a manufacturer perceives that his hold upon certain markets is loosening is, that he seeks to cut out his rival by lowering the price. To what extent the fight for supremacy in that respect will be carried depends a good deal upon the resources of the rivals. Our own manufacturer, having had the start, will probably be the stronger, and he will in certain cases endeavour, by extreme measures at first, to starve out his rival altogether. This, however, is a system of warfare that can only succeed for a time. Other foreign competitors are sure sooner or later to spring up and renew the warfare, until at last they obtain a footing from which they cannot be entirely dislodged. Then comes a time when the richer and more powerful competitor realises the fact that discretion is the better part of valour, and they seek a *modus vivendi* which has a false semblance of friendliness that time alone can smooth down. It has taken a long time for our foreign rivals to become formidable competitors in any branch of manufacturing industries. In some branches we shall probably always hold our lead, so long as the existing sources of supply of materials are what they are; but the best evidence of this country having now to share the loaf with others than the workers in the manufacturing industries of these islands is to be found in the decline in prices, the real and tangible causes of which it is the object of this work to discover.

We set out in this chapter with the axiom that " the fall in profits lowers to some extent the cost of things which are manufactured by machinery." Prices fell, as we well know, when hand-looms were superseded. The prices of travelling fell when steam superseded horses. The prices of everything fell when steam connected the chief market places of the nation, and facilitated the distribution of perishable goods. The prices of things, again, fell *pari passu* with the growth of financial institutions, founded to lend money on security. There has been an enormous development in this respect, the rivalry being as keen internationally as that among the manufacturing industries. Permanently cheaper money follows the growth of international confidence. One hundred pounds in our day can do the work which fifty years ago required many times that sum. That means a corresponding loss to the capitalist, and a proportionate lowering in the cost of everything into which the machinery of money enters as an element. With the growth of the telegraph system, money in the shape of metal has been—in proportion to the growth of operations in which money plays a part—diminishing like the dew before the rays of the sun. In other words, *confidence annihilates money.* In our day, the amount of metal money required diminishes in an inverse ratio to the increase in the magnitude of the operations. The country shopkeeper will not trust the village blacksmith with a shilling's worth of nails for his horseshoes unless he produces the coin. In the London Stock Exchange the aggregate operations of the fortnight, as shown by the Clearing House returns, reaches from one hundred and fifty to two hundred millions of pounds, all of which is settled without the intervention of one single gold sovereign. This is a demonstration that confidence annihilates money.

There is at the present time a visible and important movement in the direction of the leading commercial and financial houses of all nations striving to preserve their good name in the markets of the world. Defaulting States are at the same time seeking to reinstate their credit, and to make some atonement for the past recklessness of their borrowing. The flash of the electric telegraph keeps everyone on the alert, both as to his own financial status and that of his neighbour; it searches every crevice in the channels of commerce. The moment a weak spot develops itself it is whispered far and wide in a moment—even the journals, unjustifiable as it is, daring to give hints in such a way that the capitalist lenders put their finger on the spot in an instant. The moral and purifying effect of such a system of commercial espionage is tremendous.

A great authority on the statistics of stocks of grain, &c., &c., wrote to us some years ago that he had then gone through the stocks held for the last forty years, and found them then much the same. "London," he remarked, "when the Kingdom's imports were under three millions, had, however, as much as now, when thirteen millions are wanted." In proportion, therefore, to the quantity consumed, the stocks held in granaries were already, some years ago, about ten perhaps, very much smaller, the surplus supplies being, to a large extent, maintained afloat ready to be sent wherever required. The sources of supply, it is hardly necessary to state, have been revolutionised. California, and later India, changed all the old standards. Unnamed countries now send more than did formerly the chief sources of supply, viz., the Baltic.

Prices had been nominally much inflated up to the period of the great reaction which commenced when the fall in silver occurred, through the custom which prevailed in many branches of trade of habitually allowing deductions. The destruction of middlemen, to some extent in all branches and almost entirely in others, through the extension of the telegraph and the introduction of other facilities, enabled producers and distributors to reach the consumer with greater ease and at less cost. The growth simultaneously of competition stimulated the downward tendency of nominal prices, which became too strong for such resistance as is often brought to bear by "rings" and syndicates of producers and traders, and the victory of the public ended, as such movements often do in other departments, in the sort of rout which the decline in the price of silver ultimately brought about.

Eastern merchants foresaw that the fall in silver would stimulate exports from the East, and sold heavily in anticipation.

The use of cheques between European monetary centres has to a large extent superseded the use of gold, thus showing that greater international confidence tends to throw metallic and paper currency more and more out of employment.

All holders of silver have necessarily sustained a heavy loss, which must more or less affect adversely the prices of other things which they possessed, or that they had hitherto been purchasers of.

By the extension of the telegraph much labour is saved, in a great variety of ways. The granaries, for example, containing the surplus stocks, are now chiefly the ships themselves. England, as the largest holder and buyer for herself, gets orders for other countries from her ports-of-call, but the actual export remains insignificant. Most countries producing enough for their own consumption, it is only England, Belgium, Holland, Switzerland, and sometimes France, which are interested in the surplus supplies. One of the effects of international trade has been to greatly enlarge the area of production, and obviously the freer that trade is the better for all consumers.

THE EFFECTS UPON PRICES OF A BETTER SYSTEM OF DISTRIBUTING LABOUR.

One of the reasons why the commercial depression of the past few years has adversely affected this and other countries so much less than was the case in former times is because the facilities for distributing unemployed labour, both in this country and those to which labourers principally emigrate, have been largely extended. The extension of railways, in the first place, was the means of bettering the condition of the labourer, by conveying the surplus supply of food from one district to fill the deficiency in another, more particularly of rapidly perishable commodities. The cost now for carrying 100 lbs. of wheat from Chicago to New York is 9 cents, whereas the value of that grain was consumed in going the same distance twenty years ago. This was a distinct gain to the existing powers of production to the extent of the yield of the labour by such means set in motion.

The extension of the telegraph further aided the movement, by putting the different districts into speaking connection.

Secondly, the extension of railways, more particularly abroad, during the last twenty years or so, supplemented the distribution of food according to requirements by the distribution of labour, which is even a still more useful work from the point of view of the wealth of nations. The cheap transfer of idle labour to a point where it is wanted is a factor in production of the highest importance, and it is to be regretted that statesmen have not at all times done their best or wisest to guide the distribution of labour into the right channels.

There is little doubt in the minds of thinking economists that, in another direction, the Ministers of General Grant made a great mistake in not funding their greenbacks, and leaving to be redeemed their public bonds until a more fitting opportunity. Such a measure would have very materially hastened a recovery from the stagnation in industry which prevailed in the United States during President Grant's tenure of office. One of the great evils of a depreciated paper currency was laid bare by those errors of State policy. One of the worst effects of such a currency is to enhance retail more than wholesale prices, causing a rush of labour into distribution instead of into production. To encourage the extension of machinery for facilitating distribution is a prime necessity, no doubt, with statesmen, but the machinery having to a large extent been perfected in that country, it was surely, under the circumstances, a great error to permit the continued existence of a condition of the currency which starved the one and overfed the other.

Can it not with reason be contended that the extension of banking facilities has brought with it an important change affecting the currencies of the world, which has had the effect of placing those currencies more and more beyond the reach of the influences which affected them before banks were introduced? Whereas the circulating medium consisted almost exclusively of metal before banks were invented, now by far the larger part of the duty of that medium is discharged by bank notes, or what is called circulating credit, and by cheques, bills of exchange, and telegraphic transfers. The establishment of banks, as we have said, caused a large part of the metallic currency to be gathered together into their strong rooms, thus forming their reserves, and transferring the metal from floating currency into more or less fixed capital.

If the quantity of money in circulation can be moved about twice as rapidly, owing to improved means of transit, half the volume can be dispensed with. This applies more to international movements of gold than to domestic. Every contrivance of an economic nature which supersedes the use of metal currency dispenses with it. We live in a time when metal, both gold and silver, has been thrown out of international employment upon a larger scale than has been experienced previously during this century. The probabilities, therefore, are, that there could have been no appreciation of gold owing to its scarcity. Prices are not only depressed by a diminution in the amount of purchasing power, but by an increase in the quantity of goods. We know the quantity of goods offering in the market has largely increased of late years, owing to the much extended area of production and the increased facilities.

It is well known that the incomes of the well-to-do class, the owners of land, for instance, have been greatly reduced of late years, and consequently " the decline in the aggregate of money incomes devoted to expenditure for consumption " must have exercised a powerful influence in depressing prices.

A descent from inflation prices commenced with

the spread of the telegraph system, because it was soon found to be safer and better to do business on the ready-money system than on credit. A partial annihilation of the credit system, which has so diminished the number of bills of exchange in existence, exercised a powerful influence in depressing prices.

The cost of putting their supplies of coal on the foreign stations of the great ocean-carrying steamers has fallen about one-half during the past twelve years, the cost per ton having come down in that proportion during that period from 45s. per ton.

In 1861, J. S. Mill wrote: "But there are still extraordinary differences both of wages and of profits between different parts of the world." All this has been greatly changed during the last quarter of a century, with the inevitable result of bringing down prices. When profits are high and wages are high people can afford to pay higher prices.

Tooke wrote as follows: " And it is well known that sales made to satisfy engagements entered into beyond the means of the debtors are commonly sold at a depression as much below the fair value as *the credit prices were above the fair value.*"

The fall in silver impoverished shoals in the Eastern trade, Eastern banks, Indian pensioners; some Eastern merchants were almost swept away. Eastern banks became gigantic pawnshops. The shipping trade naturally suffered.

J. S. Mill says, p. 174, Vol. II., "Pol. Econ.":
" The cheapness of a thing is not alone measured by its money-price, but also by that price in comparison

with the incomes in money of consumers." The large
incomes of the landed proprietors of England and
Scotland, and simultaneously of all their tenants, were
falling seriously at the time of the demonetisation of
silver by Germany. In other words, the greatest industry of these islands, that of agriculture, was suffering
severely at that period, and for years afterwards, for
reasons only too well known. Simultaneously with the
fall in the prices of the products of British agriculture,
thereby reducing the money incomes of those directly
and indirectly depending upon them, these products were
being cultivated abroad over ever-increasing areas, resulting in a continuous fall in prices, until corn reached
an unprecedentedly low level of value. Had there been
no fall in the value of silver at all and no disturbance
of the gold market, a considerable fall in prices must
have been caused by these circumstances, so far-reaching
have they been in their direct and indirect effects. The
effect upon the markets of the world of so serious a
diminution of the individual incomes in Great Britain
is immeasurable, to say nothing of the influences in
the aggregate upon the agricultural interests of other
European nations, all of whom have suffered more or
less severely from the competition of the United States
in cereals; from that of Australia and other parts in
meat and wool; from that of India in cotton and tea,
which comprise some of the leading staples in which
there has been such a great fall in price.

The fall in silver induced Eastern merchants and
bankers to carry on their business on a cash basis
instead of on a credit basis, the fluctuations and unsteadi-

ness of the exchanges introducing so much uncertainty into the business as to render the cash basis preferable. A great contraction of credit was thus brought about, causing a fall in prices.

It is very important to remember that money prices rise from an increase of purchases on credit, just as they would if acted upon by purchases for cash, and that they fall by a contraction of credit, just as they would by a decline in general purchasing power, or a permanent withdrawal from circulation over a longer period of so much coined money. It is well known that the extension of the telegraph to a large extent annihilated the credit system. Every London banker will tell you that bills of exchange have become scarcer and scarcer during the last few years. To some extent, therefore, we are able to demonstrate that prices have been forced down by the withdrawal of a support which has nothing to do with the currency, and which yet exercised a potent influence in reducing values.

MONEY NOT IN CIRCULATION HAS NO EFFECT ON PRICES.

The last Bankruptcy Act exercised a powerful influence in the direction of preventing traders from making reckless speculative purchases on credit. Such purchases having the same effect on prices as if made with cash, prices would tend to fall to a more normal level, owing to a general decline of speculative purchases. Speculation in produce may be said, comparatively speaking, to have almost vanished since 1868, when harvest reports, telegrams, and other published accounts of the progress of crops, &c., informed the whole world of the position. Speculation remains in those cases where between shipment and arrival the interval is several months. Telegraphic extension has given cohesion to value all over consuming countries; it has developed ports-of-call, where cargoes await orders to go where wanted. In recent years fluctuations have been quicker and sharper. Besides, the facilities for dealing for cash offered by the extension of the telegraph caused a great diminution in the number of purchases on credit, thereby tending to cause a decline in general prices.

It will be remembered by those more familiar with financial matters, that up to the time of the Franco-German War there had been a great deal of borrowing in England, more especially by foreign States, and that the success of every new loan put into the hands of the borrower new purchasing power to the extent of the cash handed over by the agents for that loan. By this means hundreds of millions of money which had previously laid more or less dormant sprang into life, and exercised its effect upon the markets of the world, irrigating, so to speak, every commercial channel through which its fertilising power flowed, and drawing after the newly-created purchasing power a mass of new coinage, which would be maintained in circulation in proportion to the extent of the requirements. That process might very rightly be credited with causing some scarcity of gold, although no complaint of the kind was heard at the time, because more would be required; whereas the counter movement whose effects we are inquiring into would rather increase than diminish the available supply.

But the probabilities are, that the Californian gold discoveries so increased the quantity of that metal that the requirements, as far as new gold coinage was concerned, were more than satisfied, notwithstanding the exercise of the largely increased purchasing power which the borrowing of the foreign Powers referred to occasioned. Russia, it will be remembered, borrowed about that time—*i.e.*, from 1860 onwards—considerably over one hundred millions sterling, to say nothing of the operations of the United States, Italy, Spain, Turkey, Egypt, Peru, the South American Republics, &c.

What has subsequently affected the purchasing power of nations?

Heavy debts. Borrowing came to an end for the time with the Franco-German War.

Few people remember to what an extent all that borrowing was the cause of the depression that followed. Many foreign States were seriously crippled by having to impose a crushing taxation, which obviously prevents them buying our manufactures as previously. In addition, the proceeds of the loans in many cases have been employed, if not in warlike preparations, in an unproductive manner.

An examination of the process by which metal money is being relegated to the reserves of note-issuing banks, except as regards the few pounds individuals keep by them for current expenditure, might easily be pursued further; but we have said enough to show what a vast economic development has been latterly taking place, which makes for the lowering of profits and the *decline in the cost of things*. The tremendous blow at the foundations of silver as international currency struck by Germany's demonetisation of the metal gave a great speculative impetus to the operations of Eastern traders. Many of those astute people saw clearly enough what that demonetisation by Germany would soon mean upon the prices of produce in Mincing Lane. They have been the wise men of the East, and the bi-metallists the foolish ones crying in the wilderness. A voice has been raised by one set in support of a theory which appeared to them on the surface to offer a solution of the problem, but which was a mere phantom, receding, as time has shown, farther into the distance the longer it is pursued.

Another set, by far the more astute of the two, used these misguided theorists to help them to pump out a hopelessly water-logged craft, which was destined to settle further and further down into the element which no longer acknowledged its utility, and whose unsea-worthiness has caused it to be relegated to the inferior rank of a second-class power among the currencies of nations.

CHAPTER IV.

THE PRECIOUS METALS. GOLD IN ITS RELATION TO THE FALL IN PRICES.

IT is, we believe, an unfortunate fact, that the particular period of history in which the lot of this generation is cast will be looked back upon as one famed for the number of its unsound economic teachers. We not only possess no Adam Smith, Malthus, Ricardo, or John Stuart Mill, but we have been treated for years past to a steady downpour of unsound economic reasoning, the like of which we believe it would be difficult to match. Fortunately, there is an undercurrent of what we may call operative sound, though unostentatious, good sense, which in this country may nearly always be relied on, sooner or later, to close the door against the efforts of misguided theorists, however energetic.

All science, like all nature, is, with periods of pause for repose, continuously unfolding itself. The old maxims no doubt are trustworthy guides when viewed from the standpoint of the period when they were discovered and elevated into that distinguished position; but there will in most cases come a time when, like other things, they are to some extent worn out. A large proportion of the writers of any period expound their views by the light, very often, of a course of study, and often by the darkness of no study at all, which can only partially guide them in the direction of what they are seeking. We are inclined to think that the utterances of even the best informed on economic subjects have been in our time delivered, either by pen or word of mouth, too much by the light of teaching which itself requires revising, so as to bring it down to date. We find ourselves to-day, in other words, in the presence of phenomena which will not yield to an investigation undertaken altogether on the old lines. We all know how timid people with any reputation at all, whether deserved or not, are of attempting to break new scientific ground. So long as they reproduce what others of much repute have said, there is no one who dares to tell them they are wrong. Hence, we often get new reasoning on present phenomena which is sought to be explained by old maxims which only half apply. We are ourselves of opinion that reasoning of this kind has been put forward for several years past to account for phenomena which can only be satisfactorily explained by taking the hatchet and hewing a way through the economic jungle, until we discover the true causes of what we have seen.

Much has been written and said on this subject, and still even the best reputed authorities acknowledge themselves to be in considerable doubt whether their views are sound or not. In attempting to account for the fall in prices under review, we are of opinion that conclusions have been jumped to on the old lines without sufficient investigation, and that new causes were at work, and still are at work, whose operations have yet to be traced out and made as clear as the tangled influences in operation in such changes ever can be.

We have heard much about the appreciation of gold. What does this phrase mean ? Some people say the appreciation of gold is the same thing as the depreciation of other things, of the relative value of which gold is the measure. These no doubt are difficult problems, and people in consequence, as a rule, shrink from coming to close quarters with them, for fear of making gross blunders, or of showing themselves to be unsound reasoners. Such timidity is a weakness which should not hinder any man from grappling with them who is interested in getting at a true solution.

Now gold, although used chiefly to facilitate the exchange of other things, is, we need hardly say, just as much a commodity as anything else. When cotton appreciates in value it becomes dear, not because flax or indigo depreciates, but because, owing to the operation of supply and demand, you can get less of it in exchange for other things. So it can only be said that gold at any time appreciates because, owing to the operation of supply and demand, you can get less of it in exchange for other things. In other words, for anything to get dearer or cheaper something must happen to affect either way its individual intrinsic value measured in gold. To say that because some other things have fallen in value owing to the operation of supply and demand, or to diminished utility, therefore gold has appreciated, is, we believe, scientifically incorrect. Gold cannot be said to have either appreciated or depreciated unless the quantity in active operation has either materially decreased or increased, or its exchange value in relation to everything else has been affected. If it could be proved that Primrose Hill were one solid nugget, weighing one hundred millions of tons, from the moment that announcement was authoritatively made gold would depreciate in value speculatively, and people would be chary of holding any large quantity of the metal, because they would fear, naturally, that more gold might pass rapidly into circulation, thereby doubling, say, the quantity of gold, and causing a fall of one-half in its intrinsic value. But the depreciation, until more had passed into circulation, would be purely speculative. Prices, in reality, could not be otherwise than speculatively affected until an addition had been made to the number of the gold coins circulating. Over long periods of time, prices, unless affected by the operation of supply and demand, affecting each according to circumstances, remain at a level which is measured roughly by the intrinsic value of the mass of the metallic medium in active circulation.

We say roughly measured by the intrinsic value of the mass of metal in circulation, because, as we have already shown, our silver coins have been for years past purchasing more than the equivalent weight of the uncoined metal would buy. Had the mints been open to private coiners, as was the case before the Latin Union took fright, the silver coins would probably have by this time bought less of commodities than they now do, supposing always that the general collapse of prices which we have seen had come about. We are thus, as we have said, in the presence of the phenomenon that there are two values for the precious metals, and that the disparity is more sharply defined than it could be

were the free passage of the metals through the mints
unimpeded. The closing of the mints dams off the
supply from pouring into circulation, and lowers the
price per ounce of the uncoined metal. If the converse
were the case, as in a forced paper or debased currency,
the circulating coins themselves would, of course, dis-
appear. The silver tokens at present in circulation
may at the same time be said to purchase more of the
necessaries of life than they did before the downfall of
silver; and this is true; but this circumstance is accounted
for by the fact that the necessaries of life are produced
at a less cost in labour than formerly, owing to the
universal introduction of machinery where manual labour
was alone available; and that, although better machinery
is also used in the production of the precious metals,
commodities are produced with still greater facility.

If it be conceded that the intrinsic value of gold is
affected like that of other commodities, it must also be
admitted that, as we say of other articles of commerce,
they must come to market and exercise their influence
through the agency of supply before price can be
affected. Therefore gold cannot be said either to
appreciate or depreciate unless the quantity in circulation as currency, either in its own or in a representative
capacity, diminishes or increases sufficiently to affect
its exchange value. This we take to be a demonstration,
and all that can be said in attenuation of the argument
is, that the published evidence of an increase or decrease
in the supply on the one side, and an increase or decrease
in the supply of the metal from the mines on the other,
will exercise a speculative influence on its exchangeable
value in one direction or the other.

Having arrived at this point, in order to apply a test, we must discover what were the movements of gold during the period when the fall in prices was taking place; because, if we can prove that the gold in circulation did not diminish in amount in advance of the fall in prices, but only in consequence of that fall, we establish the fact that prices could not have fallen through the direct influence of an appreciation in its intrinsic value.

Gold going from hoards into active circulation, and *vice versâ*, is like grain going from the granaries to be sold at Mark Lane. In the one case, as in the other, so long as the hoards are untouched, whether of gold or of grain, prices cannot be affected, unless speculatively, through knowledge or rumour. If gold were appreciating in value through the effect of German purchases for currency purposes, it would be likely to be attracted from the chief sources of supply for the profit that was to be obtained by exchanging it for other things. The Bank of England, for instance, would experience a drain, and the value of money in London would rise. The altered position of which we have to take account in our day is, that we do not draw upon the fixed currencies, but upon the capital in the form of reserves in the banks, which, if the drain goes far enough, causes a rise in the rate of interest on capital. That advance in the rate of interest must rise above a certain level all over Europe before the fixed currencies can even be touched. In all three cases, Germany, Italy and the United States—the last-named direct from Australia— took what they wanted without disturbing any European money market in the least degree. Supposing other countries have a silver standard, that makes no difference if their paper currency is at the silver par. But nothing of the sort to which we have referred was witnessed. On the contrary, during the fourteen years from 1871 to 1884 that institution received £14,716,000 more than it lost, as the following figures show :—

GOLD.

IN. £	ON BALANCE DURING	OUT. £
7,534,000	.. 1871	
4,065,000	.. 1872	
2,034,000	.. 1873	
954,000	.. 1874	
1,681,000	.. 1875	
5,534,000	.. 1876	
—	.. 1877 ..	6,088,000
6,039,000	.. 1878 ..	—
—	.. 1879 ..	4,662,000
—	.. 1880 ..	2,911,000
—	.. 1881 ..	2,674,000
2,577,000	.. 1882 ..	—
899,000	.. 1883 ..	—
—	.. 1884 ..	266,000
£31,317,000		£16,601,000

£14,716,000 in, on balance, for the 14 years.

Where, then, did the gold come from if it were not taken from any of the great European centres? It came partly from the floating surplus supply of international currency, and partly from the hoards which had no doubt been considerably disturbed by the Franco-German War. It came, like the grain from the granaries, where there is any profit sufficient to induce the owners to bring it to market.

The question is always a debateable one whether or not, as far as the bulk of the metallic currency of Europe is concerned, any very material change took place as a direct consequence of the action of Germany in adopting a gold standard. Some people will argue that because silver fell in its gold price through Germany demonetising it, therefore gold must have appreciated through the greater demand for it. Surely it is possible to make a profit by moving stores of gold from one place to another without the article itself appreciating in value. We know that the value of silver has fallen— one very potent cause being its diminished utility, and another the large excess of supply over demand. Here are two tangible proofs, requiring us to make no further investigation.

In the case of gold there are no similarly tangible potent causes, while we think we can fully account for the fall of prices without it being necessary to search for any like influences having affected gold.

Those who have had doubts in their minds whether or not they were right in attributing the fall in prices to an alleged appreciation in gold, had probably not remembered when promulgating their views the foregoing evidence contained in the researches of Tooke and others, that in all cases they had found that a contraction of the currency always followed a fall in prices, and *never preceded it.* If that were true when European mints were open to the coinage of silver, how much more certain is it now that that is the operation of cause and effect, than when the flow of the metals through the mints was unimpeded.

We repeat that we believe that the real truth of the position is, that the amount of currency in circulation generally, in proportion to the quantity of commodities to be exchanged, has been steadily diminishing ever since the fall in prices commenced, and that in consequence, there has not only been no scarcity of gold at any time, but that the supply available for currency purposes has been steadily increasing, and going back into the hoards from which some of it was drawn by Germany.

The fact cannot be sufficiently emphasised that there is in our time but little fluctuation in the quantity of the metallic currency of countries in circulation, as was formerly the case, except under circumstances of generally rising or falling prices, as in the case under notice, and that these currencies lie, comparatively speaking, outside and beyond the influence of the effect of the interchange of commodities between nations. There was a time, and that not so very long ago, when there was much less confidence between nations than there is now. Under those former circumstances there was a much larger volume of metallic money in international circulation—chiefly silver—*in proportion* to the volume of commodities exchanged internationally than there is now. There is no doubt actually a much larger quantity of metallic money in circulation in these times than there was fifty years ago, which is a necessity, owing to the large increase in the population almost everywhere, while the volume of international transactions has increased in a still greater ratio; but, on the other hand, the development of economic science has enabled the leading nations not only domestically, but internationally, to dispense to a large extent with even the paper representatives of metallic money which were formerly employed as a medium. It is evident, therefore, that while the trade of nations has expanded enormously around the central pivot of metallic money, which consisted formerly chiefly of the coins in circulation, and in later times of the coins in circulation plus the bullion in Imperial and National Banks, which is the security at the back of the paper issues authorised by the respective Governments, the influence exercised by international trade upon the volume of coin in circulation has so declined as to justify the statement that in our day the prices of commodities are scarcely touched by either the expansion or contraction of the circulating medium, whether of coins or paper, unless, as we have before said, it be a general change either way of an unusual kind. It is true that the occurrence of a financial panic at a great centre like London would be followed by a compulsory contraction in the circulation of Bank of England notes, as was formerly frequently the case through the operation of a sustained rise in the Bank of England rate of discount; but these panics almost came to an end with the Black Friday of 1866, and for several years past there has been no longer any apprehension on that score, owing to the rapid communication which has been established between the great monetary centres not only of Europe, but between the United States, India, and other of the more important trading countries of the world.

The state of the foreign exchanges at no time during the large operations that were being carried out on behalf of the German Government indicated that any adjustment of currencies was going on in consequence of an abstraction from the active circulation. On the contrary, the gold required to enable Germany to set up a standard currency in that metal was bought precisely as if any other merchandise were being purchased in the markets of the world, and the operations were conducted at times and in seasons when it would disturb as little as possible the money markets of Europe. This proves, if it proves anything, that the gold absorbed into the circulation of Germany was taken, as we have said, either from liberated gold currency, or from private hoards and bankers' reserves, as and when it could be conveniently obtained, and that the purchases did not derange the permanent metallic currencies of the world beyond effecting a mechanical readjustment, and consequently did not disturb, through their direct influence, the general level of the prices of commodities, any more than if that gold had been dug out of the bowels of the earth in California or Australia.

In our humble opinion, conclusions have been not only erroneously arrived at that prices have fallen owing to what is called an appreciation of gold, because less of that metal is understood to have been discovered of late years; but whether less or more has been discovered does not affect the question, even if it be the fact that the supply has fallen off, *unless it can be proved that a decrease in the supply means a diminution in the volume of gold coins in circulation,* and a consequent enhancement of its value relatively to other commodities, and reflected in a general fall in the level of *all values.*

The cost of production will obviously exercise a continuously operative effect while the rate of consumption keeps pace approximately with production; but what applies to commodities which are consumed more rapidly than the precious metals applies to gold only in a qualified sense. As we have shown, the decrease of coined metals through wear and tear is very slow. When once a supply has been created, the element of cost of production plays a smaller part, as regards its influence upon the general stock, than is the case with a commodity more rapidly consumed.

The circulating medium—*i.e.,* the metals and bank notes convertible into metal on demand—are divisible into two parts, one active and the other inactive. According as trade is active or inactive, there is more money in circulation, and less in reserve or hoarded, and *vice versâ.* If the incomes of communities increase, they spend more, prices rise, and the active circulation increases, absorbing a portion of the reserves. If general incomes decrease, an opposite process commences, until the minimum of active circulation is all that is left moving, credit having contracted, bills of exchange disappearing, and hoards and bankers' reserves being at their maximum.

What has been the known effect, from time to time,

upon the mass of metal in existence as currency by the additions from the mines, allowing for the abstraction through the requirements for the arts, for loss and wear and tear? What do the authorities say on this point?

Mill says:* "Being so largely used, not only as money, but for plate and ornament, there is at all times a very large quantity of the precious metals in existence; while they are so slowly worn out, that a comparatively small annual production is sufficient to keep up the supply, and to make any addition to it which may be required by the increase of goods to be circulated, or by the increased demand for gold and silver articles by wealthy consumers. *Even if this small annual supply were stopped entirely, it would require many years to reduce the quantity so much as to make any very material difference in prices.*† The quantity may be increased much more rapidly than it can be diminished; but the increase must be very great before it can make itself much felt over such a mass of the precious metals as exist in the whole commercial world."

Here we have to note that the quantity is much more easily increased than diminished, and that, consequently, we should be more likely to witness a rise in prices from an increased quantity of metal currency than a fall from a decrease in the quantity, supposing always that the volume of the metal currency could be increased by the mints being open to private coining, which is practically no longer the case. But in both cases the movement would be so slow that the best authorities

---

* "Pol. Econ." (Mill.) Vol. II., p. 28. † The italics are ours.

agree that the aggregate of prices have been in the past raised by this particular cause *only over a long series of years.* Mill's evidence on the subject is the result of a careful investigation, and he says that "it would require many years to reduce the quantity so much as to make any very material difference in prices." This view, which is supported by even greater writers than Mill, is of itself, to our mind, a demonstration that the position taken up by those who have attempted to prove that the absorption of so much gold metal by Germany, Italy, and the United States for currency purposes caused the fall in prices is an unsound one. It will no doubt be said in reply, that no such amount as that alleged to have been absorbed by the three countries named was ever before abstracted from the available supply in so short a period. Our rejoinder to that is, *that it was taken from the hoards,* the increase or decrease of whose volume, as we have shown, does not affect prices. We shall, however, endeavour further to adduce not only negative, but positive evidence in support of that theory.

Ricardo's well-known principle is as follows:— "Gold and silver having been chosen for the general medium of circulation, they are, by the competition of commerce, distributed in such proportions amongst the different countries of the world as to accommodate themselves to the natural traffic which would take place if no such metals existed, and the trade between countries were purely a trade of barter."

That principle was no doubt applicable to the state of things as they existed when Ricardo made his examination, and as J. S. Mill says in referring to it, " few are those who, even since his time, have had an adequate conception of its scientific value." The question for those who are thinking about these questions in our day, however, is, to what extent has the scientific value of that principle been disturbed by the cause of the fall in the value of silver? We see one very material change that has taken place, and that is, that the full force of that principle of Ricardo's is no longer applicable, because one of the two precious metals has been practically dethroned, and is no longer " distributed in such proportions amongst the different countries of the world as to accommodate itself to the natural traffic which would take place if no such metals existed." Indeed, we might take up the same position with regard to both metals; for we believe that the economic changes that have been taking place, especially within the last fifty years or so, have so altered the distribution of the precious metals, that whereas formerly the nations with the largest commercial dealings employed a corresponding proportion of them, now the ratio is reversed. England, for instance, has by far the largest share of the world's trade, while her visible supply of gold is only one-fourth of that, for instance, held by the Bank of France. It is not at all unlikely that an investigation would show that those nations whose state of civilisation limits their credit in the markets of the world hold a larger proportion of the precious metals relatively to the extent of their trade. Wealth, it must be remembered, does not consist in the possession of gold, but in being in the possession of the power to purchase it. What we have to discover, then, is, what has been the effect of this inversion of Ricardo's principle, always, be it remembered, from the strictly commercial point of view ? Silver, as we know, continues to flow about the world much as it did before, only more slowly, in much smaller quantities ; but with these limitations, that its circulation on Ricardo's principle is confined to those countries which still have their mints open to its free coinage. Elsewhere it will probably in future be coined on the same principle as in England, viz., as it may be required for purely domestic wants. On this system, however much or little silver circulates in a country, the limits of that country are the barrier beyond which it will not pass, unless, which is improbable, its market value should rise beyond that at which it circulates as coin. Silver ranks, consequently, as far as currency is concerned, only upon a little better level than copper, some of which is also used to make money of. The utility of the metal having been thus diminished, its value has consequently fallen, being, besides, affected in the same direction by a growing increase in the supply. We must give due weight, however, to the fact that, as we see from day to day, the *rôle* of silver as *international currency* is not yet altogether played out. It continues to be bought and shipped, chiefly to the East, and consequently, so far as we are able to judge, the effect produced by Germany's currency action is to the extent of having displaced a certain quantity of silver from the previously existing "general medium of circulation," supplying its place, so far as the changed circumstances require, with gold. When we arrive at this point, bearing always in mind that all but two mints have been closed to its coinage, the great difficulty of determining what further change has been made commences. Here, it seems to us, investigators fight shy of the more difficult problems involving the breaking of new ground and the thinking out of new issues. But if we are to get a clear view of the new departure in the working of the world's currency, we must endeavour as we proceed to penetrate to some extent beyond the veil which hangs between us and what has been going on in the direction of modifying Ricardo's principle since silver lost the greater part of its hold upon the currency systems of the world.

If all countries had done what Germany did, the value of silver would have fallen very much lower, with the probable immediate result of all the mints in the world being closed to its free coinage, and its being relegated to the inferior position of a purely domestic currency. This has, under the pressure of circumstances, nearly come to pass already, the mints of India and the United States, as we have said, being the only ones left open to its free coinage. Had all mints been closed at once, the disturbance would have been, of course, very much greater, involving probably the failure of some banks connected with the East; but there would have been a much more rapid recovery, because the evil of the oversupply of the metal would have been cured by up-rooting it. There were, however, so many interests involved, that it was hardly to be expected that such drastic measures could be adopted, even if all other countries could have afforded to follow Germany's example, which they could not. This, however, is in our opinion what we are coming to, and it is only a question of time when there will be no free mintage of silver, or for that matter of gold either, in any country.

The demand of the bi-metallists, in fact, to have the mints of all countries open for the free coinage of silver is one of the most extraordinary which can be conceived. Had their demand been acceded to, what would have been the result at this moment? The producers of that metal would have found a market for their commodity among those more astute members of the community who understood the advantages that were to be derived from coining a depreciated metal into money, with which they could discharge indebtedness for a less sum of money than the creditor had a right to.

We take up no new position in thus advocating the interests of creditors, and leaving the producers of one particular commodity, which has been used up to a certain period of our history as currency because it was, under given conditions, suitable for that purpose, to protect their individual interests as producers as best they can with the aid of the laws of supply and demand. Why the silver-mine owners, or the proprietors of national banks, like the Bank of France, are to be protected or relieved of their surplus supply by the co-operation of other interests to save them from the loss they have incurred through having too much of the article, any more than holders of pig iron or copper, we have never been able to understand. Why should not iron merchants or copper smelters be permitted to take their product to the mint and have it coined into pence and halfpence just as well as silver-mine owners?

This view was expressed as long ago as 1840, when Mr. Tooke, in his "History of Prices," wrote as follows :* " As to the hardship or injustice of being debarred from taking the silver to the mint to be coined gratuitously (as gold is), the Cornish miner might equally complain that he has not the power of *getting a better price for his copper* by having it coined at the mint and made a legal tender than by selling it in the market. And with still more reason might the exporter of goods to Chili or Cuba declaim against the policy by which copper, which he gets in return, should be excluded not only from the mint, but from any market at all, for consumption in this country. The claim is the most absurd imaginable, if supposed to be on the part of merchants; and the objection, consequently, to a gold standard on that ground is perfectly frivolous." Mr. Tooke subsequently added the following, which is deserving the attention of bi-metallists generally, and which we hope will open their eyes to the preposterous nature of the claim they have put forward : " It is so frivolous and absurd, that it may be supposed that I have merely *imagined* such an objection. But I have known it repeatedly urged, and it is gravely stated and declaimed upon in a recent pamphlet, entitled, ' Corn and Currency; or, How Shall We Get Through the Winter? By A Merchant.' "

Here is a bi-metallist of some fifty years ago labouring under the delusion that the cure for a low price in corn

---

* Tooke's " History of Prices," p. 214.

was an edict from the Government granting permission to anybody to create superfluous currency. Another fall in prices revives the fallacy. We may here remark in passing, regarding the proposal of the bi-metallists to have silver coined and interchangeable with gold at a fixed legal ratio, that we hear of no such claim being put forward by the general public, or any section of them. It should be recorded here that a ratio of, say, 20 to 1 would not be acceptable to them. They demand the old ratio of $15\frac{1}{2}$ to 1, because no other would enable them to recoup the losses they have sustained. Can the bi-metallists engaged in trade point to an equal number of persons out of trade and in no way interested in the rehabilitation of silver who endorse their views? So far as our observation has gone, the bi-metallists are most of them either dealers in silver, or engaged in trade which is directly or indirectly affected by the fall in the value of that metal. What do recognised authorities say on that point? Mr. Tooke has the following:*— "The merchants are bound to regulate themselves by the laws as they find them; the only parties to be considered in the question of any alteration of them are the public." Nobody, we should think, would venture to contest the soundness of that proposition. That being the case, what does the claim of the bi-metallists, in a word, amount to? They are nothing more nor less than protectionists in disguise: they are, in a word, *unfair* traders. Those of them who are shareholders in Eastern banks are interested in the price of silver to

---

* Tooke's "History of Prices," p. 215.

the extent of raising the value of their capital which is
being employed in India, China, &c., to the level from
which it has fallen. If that were done and they could
" get out," they would join the great public, and would
look on with indifference. In its various forms, is not
this the mainspring of bi-metallism? Are the great
public such simpletons as to be hoodwinked with the
shallow arguments, dressed up in technical phraseology,
which seek to give a fictitious value to one commodity
more than to another, because it has in the past been
used for a purpose for which, to the same extent, it is
no longer required?

We now give some extracts which have no doubt
often been read before; but it is useful to run the eye
over them again when bringing the mind to bear upon
the special points under consideration.

" The introduction of money,"* says Mill, " is a
mere addition of one more commodity of which the
value is regulated by the same laws as that of all other
commodities." He continues: " We shall not be surprised, therefore, if we find that international values
also are determined by the same causes under a money
and bill system as they would be under a system of
barter; and that money has *little to do in the matter*,
except to furnish a convenient mode of comparing values.
All interchange is in substance and effect barter.
Whoever sells commodities for money, and with that
money buys other goods, really buys those goods with
his own commodities."

---

* " Pol. Econ." Vol. II., p. 168.

The following quotations bearing upon these points we take from the same authority:—

* " The relations of commodities to one another remain unaltered by money: the only new relation introduced is their relation to money itself; how much or how little money they will exchange for; in other words, how the exchange value of money itself is determined."

† " Money is a commodity, and its value is determined like that of other commodities, *temporarily by demand and supply, permanently and on the average by cost of production.*"

" The only new relation introduced is their relation to money itself." This means that if the cost of making any required addition to the metallic currency increases or diminishes, the relation of money to commodities *pro tanto* becomes altered. Now, seeing that prices all over the world have become more equalised by means of the telegraph and the greater facilities of communication by rail and steamship than formerly, a mere change in the distribution of the precious metals would exercise scarcely any more disturbing effect than the tidal movements to which each national currency is subjected in the regular seasons. Formerly, when these greater facilities did not exist, a large addition to any nation's active currency was preceded by the well-known cause of an advance in prices in a particular country as a result of an increase in the volume of purchasing power, thus attracting foreign commodities, and turning the

---

* Mill, " Pol. Econ." Vol. II., p. 10.   † Ibidem.

exchanges against us until the surplus currency had distributed itself according to Ricardo's law, or had retired into the reserves or hoards. In our day, the world being practically one market, and there being very little effect produced by the precious metals forced through the mints by private persons, the currencies of the world will be much steadier in volume, because the effects produced by a rise in prices will spread rapidly over the whole surface, instead of being, for some time at least, merely a local influence.

Tooke says:—" It is to be remembered at all times, that for prices generally to be permanently raised there must either be a forced issue of inconvertible paper money, or a permanent addition to the gold currency as the result of an influx of the share our country would naturally receive from an increased production of the mines; *always*, be it observed, provided *other things remain the same;* and that the rise in prices would be in proportion to that which the increase in the gold should bear to that previously in circulation."

In this statement he, of course, assumes that there is a free passage for the precious metals through the mints of all countries, and that all currencies are fed according to Ricardo's law, unhindered by any such restrictions as have since been introduced. But gold is in our day practically only coined by the Governments of the nations that have established that standard, while, as we know, all the mints but those of India and the United States have been shut to silver. In these altered circumstances, silver can no longer be forced into even temporary circulation in Europe; but the process has been reversed, and it can now instead only be *drawn into circulation* when increased facilities for the interchange of commodities necessitate an increase in the silver currency. This is as it should be. Governments should simply permit new coins to be issued in response to a demand for them, as in the case of other things. It does not at all follow that because a country maintains nominally a gold standard there is necessarily much gold in circulation. In the case of Sweden, for instance, where there is a gold standard, there is hardly any gold to be seen at all in circulation. In Germany there is no doubt much less actually circulating than people imagine, and much less was actually purchased and paid for when the change from the silver standard was made than is generally supposed.

Supposing, for the sake of argument, the gold Germany and other countries required was taken from existing active circulations of gold coins, where is it most likely that the money would have come from? No one, we suppose, would hesitate to say that between them England and France would supply by far the larger part, in which case either there would have to be an increase in the active note circulation, at all events for a time, against the security of bar gold, or the reserve of the Bank of England would run down so as to cause an advance in the value of money. We know that neither of these things occurred. There was no advance in the value of money, and no increase in the note circulation. Supposing the active circulation of gold had been affected by the requirements referred to without there being any visible disturbance, one of two things must have resulted. Either the void must have been refilled by the mint authorities being called upon to supply the deficiency, or gold must have been liberated from its functions in sufficient volume to furnish Germany and other nations with what they wanted without creating any disturbance. We hold the opinion that the required supply was in part, at all events, furnished by the gold thus thrown out of employment. Those who have jumped to the conclusion that there must have been a scarcity of gold because an exceptionally large demand arose at a time when the supply from the mines had been for some time falling off, think they see the proof of their theory in the fall in prices, an argument, we beg leave to say, which is unsound, because it belongs to the order of reasoning, as we claim to have shown, which puts the cart before the horse.

The gold requirements of the three countries referred to were satisfied quickly, whereas the fall in prices was slow. The gold having been amassed quickly, and before any great movement downwards in prices had taken place, must have left a void, if it had come out of the active circulation, which it would be necessary the mint should refill. Do we find that the English mint was called upon to refill any such void? No; on the contrary, there was less gold minted, and it continued to diminish in amount as the ten years from 1876 succeeded each other. Here is the statement from the Deputy Master of the Mint for 1885:

GOLD COINAGE.

Date.	SOVEREIGNS.			HALF SOVEREIGNS.			Total Value.
	Weight.	Number of Pieces.	Value.	Weight.	Number of Pieces.	Value.	
	oz.		£ s. d.	oz.		£ s. d.	£ s. d.
1876	846,152·264	3,294,700	3,294,705 7 6	360,049·696	2,804,000	1,401,943 10 1	4,696,648 17 7
1877	—	—	—	252,062·638	1,962,800	981,468 17 11	981,468 17 11
1878	284,119·162	1,106,361	1,106,288 19 9	297,600·928	2,317,506	1,158,780 2 2	2,265,069 1 11
1879	4,500·724	17,525	17,524 13 10	4,500·922	35,050	17,525 9 3	35,050 3 1
1880	936,334·620	3,645,877	3,645,852 18 6	129,489·494	1,008,362	504,199 14 4	4,150,052 12 10
1881	—	—	—	—	—	—	—
1882	—	—	—	—	—	—	—
1883	—	—	—	360,504·197	2,807,411	1,403,713 4 4	1,403,713 4 4
1884	452,826·068	1,763,184	1,763,191 10 0	144,031·738	1,121,600	560,823 11 7	2,324,015 1 7
1885	181,494·653	706,685	706,655 17 4	582,162·940	4,533,605	2,266,796 18 11	2,973,452 16 3
	2,705,417·491	10,534,332	10,534,219 6 11	2,130,401·653	16,590,334	8,295,251 8 7	18,829,470 15 6

AN AUTHORITY ON THE CAUSES OF THE CHANGE IN PRICES IN 1859.

In endeavouring to account for a considerable rise or fall in the price of commodities, which has been continuous in a number of the leading staples, it is always useful to ascertain what other investigators have assigned as the causes in former times. In looking through some old numbers of the *Economist,* we came across some valuable information, which we are of opinion will throw considerable light upon the causes of the fall in prices which has taken place in our time. In the number of the *Economist* for 16th April, 1859, we find the following article on

" THE ALLEGED DEPRECIATION OF GOLD AT PRESENT.

" Nothing is more curious than to observe the different degrees of confidence with which various writers speak of the depreciation or non-depreciation of gold. The language of Mr. Cobden and of M. Chevalier, though intimating a modified belief in the *present* depreciation, is one of doubt and caution. They feel the difficulty of the question, and their language is calm and philosophical. A contemporary, who disagrees with some of the remarks which we recently made on this subject, does not, however, feel any hesitation. 'Anybody,' it observes, ' who will tell us that the effect is not already perceptible in a multitude of articles—from horses to gloves or boots, from beef to brandy—we can only say keeps his purse opener than his eyes, and does not look at two sides of his shilling.' Mr. McCulloch,

on the other hand, whose practised habits of research entitle his opinions at least to attention, observes:—
'There is nothing, in truth, whatever, in comparing the prices of to-day with those of ten years ago, to entitle anyone to affirm that the value of gold and silver has undergone the smallest change in the interval.'

" Our own opinion, as we recently explained, is, that long experience is required to give us the means of ascertaining the effect of the gold discoveries on the prices of the general multitude of commodities throughout the commercial world. The effect is one which it is difficult to track with accuracy; and though we can predict the tendency of the cause, we cannot with accuracy measure its power. It is certain that no such startling and evident effects as many persons were inclined to expect when the extreme fertility of the new sources of supply was first disclosed to us have hitherto happened. We see the great difference of opinion as to those effects which still prevails. We cannot but think it wise to abstain from very confidently predicting the future when the best inquirers are disagreed respecting the present.

" Let us, however, consider the facts a little more in detail. Mr. Cobden justly observes that the prices of commodities—one with another—must still be affected by the panic of 1857. 'We are still,' he writes, ' in the eddy of the crisis, and, notwithstanding, the prices of the raw materials of our staple manufactures maintain a high value as compared with any previous period.' But this fact scarcely supports the inference which he is inclined to deduce from it. Probably at no corresponding period has there been so small a diminution in the consumption of our manufactures and in the demand for their materials. Eleven years ago our exports fell from 58 millions in 1847 to 52 millions in 1848; in 1857 they were 122 millions, and in 1858 they still amounted to 116 millions; a reduction of the same amount—six millions in both cases, but on a quantity which is now twice what it was then. The reduction per cent. in consequence of this panic is therefore only one-half what it was after the last one. We all know that the domestic demand for our manufactures is much greater than it was after the panic of 1847 : our working people are better off, our middle classes infinitely more prosperous. We need not therefore be surprised that the demand for the raw material of our manufactures has not fallen off, and that their price has not declined as much as at former analogous periods. With the facts before us we should wonder if they *had* declined as much.

" Previously to the disturbance created by the panic of 1857 the general prices of this country were carefully investigated by two very competent inquirers. The late Mr. Tooke and Mr. Newmarch discussed the subject in a singularly complete manner. The general results of their investigation were, that in all the commodities to which their attention had been directed—

" Provisions and butchers' meat alone excepted—there have been considerable fluctuations of price—fluctuations in many cases sudden and violent—during the six years 1851-56.

" That in the great articles of colonial and tropical produce—tea, sugar, coffee, tobacco, raw cotton, raw silk, and indigo—the prices at the opening of 1857 are *scarcely higher* than at the opening of 1851—allowing for the special causes of disturbance in 1857 in the articles of tea, sugar, and raw silk.

" That in butchers' meat and provisions the rise in price since 1850 has been almost continuous, until in February, 1857; the prices then prevalent are, in general terms, 40 to 50 per cent. *higher* than in January, 1851. Of the causes which have specially contributed to this rise of price there is given in Appendix iv. (page 454, *seq.*) a statement of some length.

" That in most of the raw materials of manufacture—flax, hemp, timber, sheep's wool, and especially in oils, metals, tallow, and some kinds of dyes—there has been a general tendency towards progressive rise throughout the six years, resulting in a range of prices in February, 1857, varying from 30 to 60 per cent. on the prices of January, 1851.*

" That in cotton manufactures the price of yarn and cloth are, on the whole, *lower* in 1857 than in 1851 ; and, in the case of superior kinds of cotton cloth, there is in 1857 a *reduction* of about 25 per cent. on the prices of 1851, notwithstanding a closely corresponding cost of raw cotton at the two periods—the fall of the price of the finished article indicating, it is to be presumed, increased economy in the processes of manufacture.

" That the material—bricks—principally employed in the London building trade increased in price more than 50 per cent. between January, 1851, and January, 1853, but in February, 1857, has fallen to a point very nearly the same as that at which it stood at the commencement of the table. The wages of labour, however, in the London building trades rose about 12 per cent. in July, 1853, and the advance has been generally maintained.

" That in *all* the cases in which there have been, during the six years, either fluctuations of magnitude, or a marked rise or fall of price, the changes, in the first instance at least, admit of being explained by purely mercantile reasons relating to supply and demand. In the striking instances, for example, of the increased prices in 1857 as compared with 1851 of a large class of raw materials, an explanation is at hand in each case, founded either upon a diminished supply available to meet an undiminished demand, or a stationary supply available to meet an enlarged demand :—as regards some of the most important commodities, however—raw cotton and sheep's wool, oils and metals, for example—

---

* In connection with these circumstances, the details in the Supplementary Chapter of Volume V. (page 640) should be referred to.

the immediate cause of the high price consists much more in extension of the demand than in any failure of supply.

And 'if we seek to condense into still more general terms the conclusions justified by the course of prices since 1851,' we may say that—

"The groups of commodities which exhibit the most important instances of a rise of price are the raw materials most extensively used in manufacture, and the production of which does not admit of rapid extension; and, second, that the groups of commodities in which there is little, if any, rise of price in 1857 as compared with 1851 are articles of colonial and tropical produce, the supply of which, drawn from a variety of sources, does not admit of being considerably and expeditiously enlarged.

"We cannot but think, therefore, that it is somewhat rash and peremptory to pronounce that there is any depreciation of gold at present. Certainly there has been no rise of prices since two of the most able statistical writers in this country arrived at the above conclusions. All that can be said is, that the fall of general prices since that time is not so great as might have been anticipated. But, as we have shown, even this fact may be easily explained from the peculiarities of the present period, as compared with previous similar ones."

In the same number of the *Economist* appears the following:—

"A very intelligent correspondent has written to us respecting the price of silver, and we printed his letter on the 26th March. The most elaborate investigation of the recent price of silver which we have met with is that of McCulloch, in the article in the 'Encyclopædia Britannica,' to which we have repeatedly referred:—'It has been attempted,' he says, 'to show that gold has fallen in value, by alleging that the value of silver, as compared with it, has increased. *But a rise may take place in the comparative value of silver without its being occasioned by a corresponding fall in the value of gold.* The value of silver is affected by a variety of circumstances peculiar to itself; and if it has really increased during the last half-dozen years, such increase may be satisfactorily accounted for by the extraordinarily increased demand for it in the East. It is, however, very doubtful whether there has been any rise in the value of silver as compared with gold. We subjoin an account of the price of silver per oz. in London in the months of March, July, and November annually since 1852, viz.: —

Years.	March.	July.	November.
	d.	d.	d.
1852	60⅛	60¼	61⅞
1853	61⅜	61½	61⅞
1854	61⅞	61¾	61½
1855	60⅞	61½	60⅞
1856	60	61¼	62⅛
1857	61¾	61⅝	61½
1858	61⅝	—	—

Price per Ounce.

" 'It does not appear from this table that the price of silver has risen during these seven years. It appears to have fluctuated much less than might have been anticipated, its extremes being 60 and 62⅛, making its value, as compared with that of standard gold (at £3. 17s. 6d. per oz.), as 15·5 to 1 and 14·97 to 1; but at an average of the entire period there has been no sensible variation.'

"This elaborate statement entirely confirms the view taken in our former article. The quotations of silver there given were those for the month of March in each year. We have reason to believe that in March, 1856, there were considerable fluctuations in the price of silver. It will be found quoted in our SUPPLEMENT of 24th January, 1857, at from 60 to 61 for that month; but slight fluctuations of this sort cannot affect a general argument. Since our former articles were written there has been a considerable rise in the price of silver, in consequence of the stimulated demand for exportation to the East."

Gold, it is true, has here paid for commodities, and will, as a rule, be sold again whenever it exceeds the needs of those who use it; but it is no less true that many large provincial houses are compelled to hold a large amount of gold, and fix the interest on it, so as to render themselves independent of other sources of supply in case circumstances should suddenly arise necessitating a conversion of securities into cash, which perhaps the stock markets would not admit of.

It was recognised years ago that the passage of the precious metals from one country to another was determined to a greater extent than had been supposed by the condition of the money market. The precious metals, in fact, can enter a country for investment upon a large scale without disturbing prices at all, and leave it again without either affecting them. The prices of the securities invested in would be raised or sold, as the case might be, but the prices of commodities would not be in the least affected.

How little some of the bi-metallists have cared or even thought about the interests of the community in their efforts to forward their own interests is seen in the fact that their demand to have silver rehabilitated could only be granted at the expense of a large outlay of money. Many no doubt have advocated the adoption of such a course through sheer ignorance, while others have done it knowing that it was the only means by which they could recover what they had lost. How little they have cared to see their theory carried into practice in principle is seen by their steady adherence to the ratio of $15\frac{1}{2}$ to 1. Any other ratio, such as 20 to 1, which is nearer what it is now, would not restore to them the losses incurred by the depreciation of their capital employed in the East. What impartial bi-metallist, for example, could pretend to support the bi-metallic theory after having further read the following ?

For years past some of the bi-metallists have been advocating the maintenance of prices at the level from which they have fallen during the last ten years, as if there is any particular virtue in prices continuing at a high level. Will a locomotive do its work any better because the coal costs 30s. a ton instead of 16s. ? Is there not a direct loss sustained in maintaining, say, sixty millions of metallic currency in a country when thirty millions, with prices reduced one-half, will suffice to exchange precisely the same quantity of commodities ? And is not a community so much the poorer for having to maintain in circulation a larger proportion of its capital than there is any necessity for ? Nothing is clearer than the absurdity of the struggle which some of these bi-metallists have been engaged in to maintain what they call "the stability of values." Was ever such a thing heard of as forming an association to maintain "the stability of values"?

Silver is just as available now as it would be if there were a fixed legal ratio, the only difference being that the ratio is now fixed by the market, which prevents debtors escaping from their liabilities at the expense of their creditors.

In the *Nineteenth Century* for June, 1886, Mr. Sassoon draws attention to Mr. Mulhall's statement in his "History of Prices," that "the quantity of silver is now only nineteen times that of gold, whereas in 1850 it was thirty-three times, and yet, *strange to say*, silver has fallen." In what consists the strangeness in the face of the fact that the effectiveness of one of the essential elements in value, viz., utility, has been impaired? It matters not how much or little of a thing exists, if it is no longer wanted by people on the same scale as before its commercial value must inevitably fall.

Mr. John Wilson says:—"It is obvious that the smaller the quantity of coin which can be rendered efficient for currency purposes, consistent with the safety of public and private interests, the better for all." The same authority wrote in the *Economist* of March, 1845: "If trade increased, a greater number of labourers became employed and more wages were paid; and if commodities *rose in price*, the public would find that they required to keep a larger portion of their capital *in money* to answer those new calls; the circulation would increase and deposits decrease."

CHAPTER V.

THIS CHAPTER CONTAINS CHIEFLY POSITIVE EVIDENCE IN SUPPORT OF THE POSITION PREVIOUSLY TAKEN UP.

WE think the reader who is not hopelessly prejudiced in favour of what we may call the double-standard bi-metallic party will, after having read carefully what is contained in the preceding 87 pages, begin to feel that the foundation upon which Mr. Goschen's views as to the cause of the fall in prices under review were based is not quite as firm as when he started with us on this little expedition. We are well aware that in putting our view of the case into such shape as we have been able we have been guilty of much reiteration. It is very difficult to avoid it. In this respect anyone may, we think, be held well excused if only he succeed, to some extent, in disentangling some of the knots into which this question has been dragged by the superheated efforts of many persons whose judgments were not under that kind of guidance which afforded a fair chance of their going straight.

We bring forward again, and in more detail, the position taken up by Mr. Goschen at the Bankers' Institute, because we think the reader will now have got into his mind the other side of the argument, and will be better able to see the force of the positive evidence as to the true causes of the fall in prices which we shall subsequently produce.

Mr. Goschen estimated that £200,000,000 had been absorbed by Germany, Italy, and the United States. His deduction was that the estimated annual production of £20,000,000 had thus been absorbed; that the world's requirements were to that extent cut off, and that the metal had in consequence so appreciated as to account for the fall in prices. That is the argument.

Mr. Goschen, in his address to the Institute of Bankers, delivered April 18th, 1883, said: "But it is not sufficient to state that the total supply of gold available for the needs of circulation in the gold-using countries of Europe has been absorbed. This additional and extraordinary demand falls upon a supply of £20,000,000, which has to furnish the wear and tear of the coinage, and the total amount used for the purposes of art and manufacture, besides the purposes of circulation." Further on we read, "Economists will accordingly ask themselves what result, if any, is such a phenomenon likely to have produced? I think there is scarcely an economist but would answer at once —'It is probable, it is almost necessary, it is according to the laws and the principles of currency, that such a phenomenon must be followed by a fall in the prices of commodities generally. Just as a large amount of gold poured into Europe in 1852 and subsequent years created a rise in prices, so the counter-phenomenon must produce a fall.'" Then Mr. Goschen goes on to remark, "It is a very curious coincidence that while tea, coffee, and sugar have fallen so materially, what we may call the luxuries of the working man—tobacco, spirits, and beer—have not fallen, or, at all events, not in the same proportion."

Mr. Goschen, in a letter to the *Times* of the 7th of May, which he said was a brief summary of the argument he used in his address at the Bankers' Institute, delivered on April 18th, 1883, states:—"It is a received axiom that prices of commodities are affected by changes in the volume of the circulating medium in which they are expressed. The late strain on the common stock of gold must, therefore, have had some result. It must have caused a general decline. Examined by the test of present prices, these deductions are borne out by facts. A general fall has occurred, though exceptional circumstances have maintained some prices."

Mr. Giffen said: "I think there is a permanent appreciation in the value of the sovereign." Mr. Giffen went on to say: "It would be of great interest to find out the precise method by which the fall would be brought about when gold has become scarcer and scarcer. If that had been gone into, it might have been apparent that where you ought to look for the fall in prices first is in those wholesale commodities which are dealt with in the great markets of the world, the commodities upon which bankers are in the habit of advancing. It is there we ought to expect first to see a fall of prices *as the result of the scarcity of gold.*"

With the exception of what we shall put together in the form of a summary, we shall now close the argumentative part of our task, and simply bring forward evidence which we have collected from time to time as it has appeared in print in support of the position we have taken up in the first four chapters.

In the *Contemporary Review* for October and

November, 1887, Mr. David A. Wells, with a clear and sound perception of the real agencies which had been at work in lowering prices, set himself the task of examining each article separately. Mr. Wells, in his article on the fall in prices, premises his investigation with remarking that " it is a universally accepted canon, alike in logic and common sense, that extraordinary and complex agencies should never be invoked for the explanation of phenomena so long as ordinary and simple ones are equally available and satisfactory for the same purpose." The fall in the prices of the articles referred to, as Mr. Wells says, is thoroughly capable of explanation, and we recommend the explanations as " ordinary and simple ones" to those economists who so persistently " invoke complex agencies," with the result that they worry the scientific world with the everlasting sound of their fog-horns.

" What these agencies have been, how they have acted, and what disturbing influences they have exerted on the world's prices, on the world's industries, commerce, and consumption, and on pre-existing relations of labour and capital, will, when fully told, constitute one of the most important and interesting chapters of political economy and commercial history. Such a complete exposition it is not at present proposed to attempt; but the following statement of results, derived from a study of what may be termed the recent production and price experiences of a considerable number of important commodities, will, it is thought, better contribute to an understanding of the situation, and to a solution of the difficult economic problems involved in it, than any other method hitherto adopted.*

---

* " A general movement in prices is the resultant of a number of particular movements, and in these particular movements, again, we find the proximate causes of the distribution of the industrial forces of the world, and of the wealth which these forces create."—J. S. Nicholson, *Professor of Political Economy, University of Edinburgh, &c.*

" Sugar.—The commodity of prime importance in the commerce and consumption of the world which appears to have experienced the greatest recent decline in price is *sugar*, which has fallen to a lower rate than has ever been known in the history of modern commerce; the wholesale price of fair refining sugars having been more than 114 per cent. higher in 1880 than in the first half of the year 1887.*

" Now, while improved methods of manufacture and greater and cheaper facilities for transportation have undoubtedly contributed to such a result, it has been mainly due to an apparent desire, as M. Léroy-Beaulieu has expressed it, on the part of the Governments of France, Germany, Austria, Belgium, Holland, Italy, and Russia, 'to make their national sugar industry the greatest in the world,' by stimulating the domestic production of this commodity by the payment of extraordinary bounties on its exportation to other countries; or, in other words, by competing with one another in paying large sums for the purpose of speedily getting rid, at little or no profit, of one of the most valuable and highly-desired products of human industry.

" On the other hand, in order to neutralise to some extent the exceptional advantages enjoyed through such an economic policy by the producers of beet-sugar in Europe, some of the cane-growing countries have felt obliged to encourage, by subsidies or tax exemptions, their own sugar-production. In both Brazil and the Argentine Republic the manufacturers of cane sugar have obtained a guarantee from the State of a five to six per cent. return on their capital invested, while all the machinery needed in this industry may be imported free of duty. In the Spanish West Indies the Home Government has finally (1887) felt compelled to relinquish the export duties on sugars—the produce of Cuba and Porto Rico—which have long been regarded as almost indispensable on account of revenue necessities; while in South Africa and Australia the production of sugar has also been encouraged to such an extent, that both of these countries

---

* How continuous and regular has been the decline in the price of sugars in recent years is shown by the following table, which exhibits the average price of fair refining sugars in bond (or free of duty) in New York from 1880 to July, 1887, inclusive :—

1880, 5·08 cents.	1885, 3·06 cents.
1882, 4·53 cents.	1886, 2·92 cents.
1884, 3·31 cents.	1887 (lowest to July), 2·37½.

will hereafter be undoubtedly included among the number of important sugar-exporting regions. In Central America, the British and Dutch West India Islands, Guiana, and India (which last produces more sugar than any other country) production has not as yet been artificially encouraged, and, with the exception of the levying of export taxes in certain localities, neither have any impediments been placed in the way of the natural growth of production. But, at the same time, it cannot be doubted that the recent increased facilities for transportation and communication have, as before pointed out, been in the nature of a stimulus to the production of sugar in common with all other commodities, and have opened up large and fertile sections of the earth which a quarter of a century ago were practically inaccessible.

" Under such conditions the increase in the production of sugar entering into the world's commerce and available for general consumption has been extraordinary. Mr. Sauerbeck estimates the increase from 1872-73 to 1885-86 to have been 68 per cent. Other authorities estimate the increase from 1853 to 1884, exclusive of the product of India and China, to have been at the rate of 30 per cent. for each decade, or about 100 per cent. compounded. In the Hawaiian Islands, where a remission of duties on sugars exported to the United States is equivalent to an export bounty of about 100 per cent., the domestic production has increased from about 12,000 tons in 1875 (the year before the duties were remitted) to 110,000 tons in 1885— an increase in eleven years of 750 per cent. The part that beet-root sugar has played in this increase is shown by the circumstance that, while in 1860 the proportion of this variety to the whole sugar product of the world (commercially reported) was less than 20 per cent., the product for 1886-87 is estimated as in excess of 55 per cent. ; Germany alone having increased her product from about 200,000 tons in 1876 to 594,000 tons in 1880-81, and to 1,155,000 tons in 1884-85 ; while the increase of the beet-sugar product in the other bounty-paying States of Europe was not disproportionate.

" Of this extraordinary increase of product as large a proportion as foreign markets would take was, as a matter of course, exported, in order to obtain the benefit of the Government bounties on exports ; the sugar-export of Germany alone increasing from about 500,000 cwts. in 1876 to over 6,000,000 cwts. in 1885, and with every increase of exportation the Government disbursements on account of export bounties increased proportionally. The export bounty paid by Russia is estimated to have been as high at one time as £6. 8s. per ton ; and that of France as between £7 and £8, entailing a present direct and indirect tax (French colonial sugar being admitted to the home market at reduced import rates), according to estimates recently presented by M. Dauphin in the French Chamber of Deputies, of £3,280,000 per annum. In Germany, the amount paid in the way of subsidies on sugar was estimated by Deputy Gehlert, in a speech in the German Reichstag in 1886, as having up to that time approximated £8,000,000 ; while for the year 1885, £2,000,000, it was claimed, would be necessary, or an amount equal to the total wages paid to all workmen in all the German sugar refineries. As might also have been expected, the profits of producers, and more especially of the sugar-refiners working under the bounty (export) system, were at the same time enormously increased. In Germany, the largest and best-managed beet-sugar manufactories divided for a series of years dividends to the extent of 60, 70, 90, and in one instance 125 per cent. per annum on the capital invested ; * and corresponding results were also reported in Austria, Russia, France, and Belgium. How rapidly and extensively sugar has declined in price, consequent upon such an extraordinary and unnatural increase in production, has already been pointed out. How much of disaster this decline has brought to great business interests and to the material prosperity, and even the civilisation, of large areas of the earth's surface will be made a subject of future notice.

" WHEAT.—The next important commodity to the recent production and price experiences of which attention will be asked is wheat. The average price of British wheat for the last week in July, 1882, was

---

* " By a law passed in 1869 it was assumed that it took $12\frac{1}{2}$ centners of beet-root to give one centner of crude sugar, and a tax was levied on this basis, and a corresponding drawback allowed on exported sugar. Since then great improvements have been made in the process of manufacturing, so that but $10\frac{1}{2}$ centners of roots are necessary to produce one centner of sugar, instead of $12\frac{1}{2}$ as formerly ; but the Government continued to grant a drawback on the basis of $12\frac{1}{2}$. The export drawback thus became an enormous premium to the producers, and the German manufacturers have been enabled to supply all Europe with cheap sugar; till, to protect themselves, the other States have had to increase their duties on the imports of foreign sugar."— *Report of United States Department of State by Commercial Agent Smith*, Mayence, January, 1887.

50s. per imperial quarter. For the corresponding dates in 1885 it was 32s. 11d., and in 1886, 31s. 3d. per quarter ; * which last quotation was the lowest since average market prices have been officially recorded.†

" The average price of wheat in the English markets for the decade from 1870 to 1880 was 43 per cent. higher than the average of 1886 ; and the average price from 1859 to 1872 was 68 per cent. higher than the average of 1886.

" An analysis of the comparative prices of wheat in the United States furnishes corresponding results ; the average price of No. 2 spring wheat having declined in the Chicago market from $1·10 (gold) in 1872 to 76½ cents in 1886, and 67 cents in July, 1887 ; a price equivalent to 29s. per quarter in the harbour at Liverpool, or 86 cents per bushel, cost, freight, insurance included. This is about the lowest price ever reported. The average annual export price of wheat for the whole country declined from $1·24 per bushel in 1880, to 86·2 cents in 1885, and 87 cents in 1886. The average price of wheat in Chicago from 1872-78 was $1·04 (gold), and the decline to the average price of 1886 was about 28 cents, representing a loss to the American producers of wheat on an average crop of at least $150,000,000 per annum. For such results an all-sufficient explanation would seem to be found in the circumstance that all investigation shows that the comparatively recent increase in the world's supply of food has been greatly in excess of the concurrent increase of the world's population ; that there has been in the last decade a large increase in the area of land devoted to the cultivation of cereals ; an increase (due to better methods of tillage) in the average product per acre ; and an immense increase in the facilities for transportation, coupled with a greatly reduced cost, which has made product more accessible and accordingly more available for distribution. The most salient points of the evidence tending to these conclusions are as follows : The cereal production of the United States increased from 932,752,000 bushels in 1862 to 2,992,881,000 in 1884 ; and in acreage from 34,594,381 to 136,292,766 ;

---

* *Economist.*

† The Eton record gave only 26s. 9¾d. per quarter as the price for the year 1761, when reduced to Winchester bushels ; but there is no certainty that the average for the entire year was even in that one market as low as that, and still less that the price was as low in more than one hundred and fifty English market towns as it was in 1886.

or in the respective ratios of 452 and 338 per cent. respectively. The average wheat production of the United States for the five years from 1881 to 1885 inclusive was 436,000,000 bushels; while for the ten years preceding—some of which supplied the heaviest demands for exportation ever experienced—the average was only 366,000,000 bushels. According to Mr. Neumann Spallart, a German statistician of repute, the production of cereals in Europe doubled from 1869 to 1879; and in the case of Russia her exports of wheat increased from 36,565,000 bushels in 1880 to 67,717,000 in 1884. According to figures of the United States Bureau of Agriculture, the average production of wheat in Europe for the five years from 1875 to 1881, inclusive, ' increased some 50,000,000 bushels over the average of the ten years preceding, which included several seasons of unusually low yield in Western Europe.' In 1862 the United States exported breadstuffs to the value of $24,000,000; in 1872 the corresponding value was $87,000,000; and in 1880, $288,000,000; and if since this latter year there has been a decline in the *value* of American cereal exports, it cannot be attributed to any impairment of ability to produce and export, if sufficient inducements existed.* While, therefore, it is clear that the comparative product of the heretofore great wheat-producing countries has not diminished, recent experiences are also making it evident that the world is hereafter to derive important supplies of wheat from sources which a few years ago did not exist, or were regarded as of little importance. For example, British India, which in 1880 exported only 13,896,000 bushels, and whose increase of wheat exports appears to be coincident with the increase of the railway mileage of the country, in 1885 exported 39,312,000 bushels. During the same period Australia and New Zealand, in which a rapid growth of population inevitably tends to divert agricultural industry from wool-producing to wheat-growing, increased their exports from 13,999,000 bushels in 1880 to 19,466,100 in 1885; and the Argentine Republic, from 5,772 bushels in 1881 to 3,986,000 in 1884. All the indications are, furthermore, that the increase of wheat supplies from new sources is likely to be continuous and of great magnitude: from India, whose

* Of the respective wheat crops of the United States for the years 1884-5-6, thirty per cent.—in the form of wheat and flour—has been exported; the largest proportion ever recorded, except during the era of crop failures in Western Europe— *i.e.*, 1878-82.

internal and foreign commerce is yet only in its infancy, but. is
developing with extraordinary rapidity under the influence of railroad
construction; * from the great wheat region of Manitoba, to open
which the Canadian Pacific Railroad was mainly constructed; from
Algeria and Northern Africa, which, once the granaries of the Roman
world, are now, for the first time for centuries, contributing something
to the world's surplus of cereals; and from the South American States
of the Argentine Republic and Chili, where extraordinary railroad
construction is rapidly drawing an extraordinary European immigration
to the finest of wheat-lands, which so recently as 1880 were practically
inaccessible. Great, also, as is the present wheat production of the
United States, Mr. Atkinson has shown that all the land at present in
actual use in that whole country for growing maize or Indian corn,
wheat, hay, oats, and cotton is only 272,000 square miles, out of
1,500,000 miles of arable land embraced in its present national domain;
and also that the present entire wheat crop of the United States could
be grown on wheat-land of the best quality selected from that part of
the area of the State of Texas, by which that single State exceeds the
present area of the German Empire.

" In short, it would seem as if the world in general, for the first
time in its history, had now good and sufficient reasons for feeling free
from all apprehensions of a scarcity or dearness of bread. But while
this is certainly a matter for congratulation, are there not, on the
other hand, reasons for apprehension of serious disturbances to the
material interests of that large part of the world's population engaged

---

* " There is nothing more remarkable in the history of railway enterprise than
the development of the traffic that has occurred on Indian railways within the last
ten years, to go no further back. In 1876 the total quantity of goods traffic carried
on all the railways of India was 5,750,000 tons. In 1886 the quantity was about
19,000,000 tons. In the year 1876 the mileage open was 6,833 miles, so that the
volume of goods traffic carried per mile was about 800 tons. In 1886 the mileage
open was 12,376, so that the average volume of traffic carried per mile was over 1,500
tons. The aggregate volume of traffic in the interval had fully trebled, and the
average traffic carried per mile open had almost doubled. Notwithstanding these
remarkable results, the traffic which has been developed on the railways of India is
less, in proportion to the population, than that of any country in the world. This is
especially the case in reference to goods traffic, which only represents some 0·05 of a
ton per head of the population, as compared with three tons per head in Canada, and
over seven tons per head in the United Kingdom. But the goods traffic of India is likely
to develop very rapidly in the future, and especially in agricultural produce, of which
only about 4,000,000 tons are now annually transported, as compared with 75,000,000
tons in the United States for less than a fourth of the population."—*Bradstreet's*
(*N.Y.*) *Journal.*

in agriculture, from the continued abundant production and decline in the price of their products ?

" The effect of the extensive fall in prices of agricultural products during the last decade has, as already pointed out, been most disastrous to the agricultural interests and population of Europe. It has reduced farming in England and Germany to the lowest stage of vitality, and has had less, but similar, effects in France, Italy and Belgium. It has brought almost to bankruptcy the sugar-producing interests in the West Indies and the Dutch East Indies, and threatens the continuance of productive industries, and even of civilisation, in these countries.* In 1880, 44 per cent. of the entire population of the United States were engaged in agriculture, and less than 7 per cent. in manufactures; and since the year 1820, or for a period of sixty-six years, the proportion between the agricultural and non-agricultural exports of this country has been remarkably steady, the average for the former for the whole of this period having been about 78 per cent. Up to the present time there has been little tendency to change in these proportions ; but if the continued fall of prices of agricultural products in the United States and other countries should compel their farming populations to seek other employments, what other employments are open to them ? That the world will ultimately adjust itself to all new conditions may not be doubted ; but what of the period pending adjustment ? †

---

* " In consequence of the low prices of sugar in Europe and America, owners of plantations, and their lessees, have speculated to such an extent, that they have placed themselves on the brink of an abyss, and it is feared that this will totally stop the production of sugar in Java. This event would be in every way a great catastrophe. It would at once throw half-a-million of Javanese labourers out of employment, who would increase the already enormous number of Malay pirates."—*Journal des Fabricants de Sucre*, October, 1886.

† A recent writer in the *Quarterly Review* broadly contests the views above expressed respecting the prospective increasing production and continued low prices for wheat, and endeavours to prove that "it has been too hastily assumed that, in the struggle for existence among wheat-growers, the British, the best farmers in the world, will not be amongst the fittest who will survive." In support of this conclusion, the writer starts with the proposition that the returns of the cost of growing wheat in Great Britain, collected in 1885, make the average about £8 per acre, and venturing the opinion that, with the general reduction of the rents of British farming-lands that have already taken place, and the practice of increased economies on the part of British farmers, they can grow wheat with a profit of 40s. and 45s. a quarter (although the average price of British wheat has not for some years reached that level), next assumes that growers " in all parts of the world—with the doubtful exception of India—cannot possibly keep up the present acreage of wheat at the recent or any lower range of prices." The writer further concludes, from an exami-

" MEAT.—The price of meat, according to the statistics of English
markets, exhibits no material decline, comparing the average prices
of 1867-77 and of 1878-85. But during the years 1885 and 1886

---

nation of American statistics, which he abundantly offers, that the area of wheat
acreage in the United States is diminishing, and that the average farm value of wheat
in that country for the years 1884-86 was about 33s., "which cannot," he says,
" yield a satisfactory profit under the most favourable circumstances."

The following reply to the conclusions of this writer in the *Quarterly*, so far as
they relate to the United States, which appeared in the columns of the *New York
Commercial Bulletin* (May, 1887), strikingly illustrates how different the situation
appears to a writer equally competent to discuss the question, when viewed from a
trans-Atlantic standpoint:

" These guesses about the cost of wheat-producing in this country are highly
interesting. Probably they will interest no one else so much as the American
farmers, who know that they do not know, and have a strong impression that other
people cannot tell them, the exact cost of raising wheat per acre. Very few of them
produce any one crop under such circumstances that they can actually compute, in
dollars or days' labour, what that separate crop costs them ; and fewer still know what
they add to the value of their land by improvements, or take from it by exhaustion
yearly. But one thing a great many of them do know—that they are going to raise
more wheat next year than they did last, as they raised more last year than the year
before ; and they have been selling wheat for several years at about 45 cents per
bushel in great regions like Kansas, Minnesota, and Dakota, and yet the business is
found so far profitable that the acreage in these very States enormously increases.
It is supposed that Dakota, which produced 22,800,000 bushels in 1880, and 22,000,000
bushels three years ago, will produce 30,000,000 bushels in 1887."

[In 1880 the crop area of the State of Kansas was about 8,000,000 acres ; for
the present year (1887) the area planted is believed to be in excess of 16,000,000 acres.]

" The farmer in this country is at the same time a land-improver and a land-
speculator in most of the wheat-growing States. He takes possession of a farm
under the Homestead Law by pre-emption or by purchase from corporations, the land
costing him so little that a single good crop or two pays for it outright. Then he
puts into it labour of his own, and of men hired, which he could not otherwise utilise
at all, and the cost of which he cannot compute, and thus adds year after year to its
value. The farmer who runs into debt can tell what his land costs him yearly, but
such are not the majority. Most farmers get a living out of the land for themselves
and families, to begin with, and make some improvements besides, and meanwhile are
gaining more, without any effort, than by all their labour; for while a farmer is
raising four or five crops, a settled State or county grows up about him. Towns and
cities start from the ground. Railroads and manufacturing establishments come to
enhance the value of his land. In a few years the ground that he bought for $1·25
to $5 per acre comes to be worth in market price $10, $20, or $30 per acre. Land
settled by men who are yet in their prime averages in value over $20 per acre for the
entire State of Iowa, or $13 for the entire State of Minnesota, or $10 for the entire
States of Kansas and Nebraska. That means for the owners of only a small farm a
yearly saving which not many wage-owners are able to accomplish, and in all the
more successful selections of land the increase in value, and the consequent return for
labour, are far greater.

" Just as long as this occupation of new land and development of new territory
are possible in this country, the most scientific calculation of the cost of growing
wheat will have as much to do with its continued production or with its average
price as it has to do with the height of mountains in the moon. Wheat-growing
will continue, and the yield in this country will greatly exceed the demand, and an
enormous surplus will be annually offered for sale at prices with which British
farmers cannot easily compete, where the cost of growing wheat averages about ' $40
per acre.' "

the decline was very considerable, and extended also to most other animal products. The percentage of fall in the carcase prices of different kinds and quantities of meat in London, as given by the *Economist* of November 27, 1885, was, in comparison with the prices for 1879, as follows:—For inferior beef, 43 per cent.; prime beef, 18 per cent.; prime mutton, 13 per cent.; large pork, 22 per cent.; middling mutton, 27 per cent.

" The immediate cause of this decline was undoubtedly the new sources of supply of live animals and fresh meats that have been opened up to Europe, and especially to Great Britain, from other than European countries; the value of the imports into Great Britain from North America of live animals having increased from £217,000 in 1876 to £4,596,000 in 1885; of fresh meat from £390,000 to £2,364,000; and of fresh meat from Australia and the River Plate (transported through refrigeration) from £178,000 in 1882 to £1,170,000 in 1885; a total increase of from £605,000 in 1876 to £8,130,000 in 1885. The ability of the three countries named to increase their exports of meat during such a brief period to such an enormous extent constitutes of itself a demonstration of increased production, and of the diminished price that is the invariable accompaniment of a surplus seeking a market. The decline in the average export price of salt beef in the United States was from 8·2 cents per lb. in 1884 to 6 cents in 1886 (26 per cent.); of salt pork from 8·2 cents to 5·9 cents (27 per cent.); of bacon and hams from 9·6 cents to 7·5 cents; and of lard from 9·4 cents to 6·9 cents. In the case of lard oil, an exceptionally great decline in price in recent years—*i.e.*, from an average of 94 cents per gallon (Cincinnati market) in 1881-82 to a minimum of 48·8 cents in 1886—is claimed to be due mainly to the large production and more general use of vegetable oils; cotton-seed oil in the United States, and palm and cocoa-nuts oils in Europe. The effect of the increased quantity and cheapness of these vegetable oils has been especially marked in England, France, Italy, and Germany; and has also undoubtedly influenced the price of tallow, the decline in which in English markets, comparing the average prices of 1867-77 with those of 1886, has been 31 per cent., while in the United States the price for 1884-85 was the lowest on record.

"CHEESE.—American cheese experienced an extraordinary decline in price, from 12 and 13 cents in 1880 to 8⅜ and 10½ cents in 1885; and as the American contribution of this article of food to the world's consumption has constituted in recent years a large factor, the world's prices generally corresponded with those of the American market. This decline in the United States was due mainly to increased production; the relative prices of butter and cheese during the year 1880-81 being so much to the advantage of the latter, that large quantities of milk which had previously gone to the creameries to be made into butter found their way into factories to be made into cheese; and for the years 1883, 1884, and 1885 the annual receipts at New York city averaged 25 per cent. in excess of the receipts for 1880. Demand for export at the same time largely fell off, and so assisted in the decline of prices; the same influences having also apparently prevailed to a degree in other cheese-producing countries, the amount recognised by the trade as supplied to the great cheese-consuming countries, Great Britain, the Continent of Europe, and South America, having increased from 1880 to 1884 to the extent of 14 per cent.

"FISH.—The year 1884 in the United States was notable for a plethora of all kinds of dry and pickled fish on the one hand, and of extremely low prices of such commodities on the other; mackerel having touched a lower price in the Boston market than for any year since 1849, while for codfish the price was less than at any time since the year 1838.

"COFFEE AND TEA.—The decline in recent years in the price of each of these great staple commodities has been almost as remarkable as has been the case with sugar; coffee having touched the lowest prices ever known in commerce in the early months of 1886, the price of 'ordinary,' or 'exchange standard No. 5,' having been 7½ cents per lb. in January of that year in the New York market; while, according to Mr. Giffen, the decline in the price of tea, comparing 1882 with 1861, has been greater than that of sugar, or, indeed, of almost any other article. In both cases the decline would seem to find a sufficient explanation in a common expression of the trade circulars: 'Our supplies have far outrun our consumptive requirements.' In the case of coffee, the total imports into Europe and the United States, comparing the receipts of the year 1885 with 1873, showed an increase of 57 per cent. ; while the increase in the crops of Brazil, Ceylon, and Java during the same period has been estimated at 52 per cent. Subsequent to January, 1886, the price of coffee, owing to a partial failure of the Brazil crop, rapidly advanced more than 150 per cent., ' ordinary ' or ' exchange ' standards having sold in New York in June, 1886, at 22 cents per lb.—the highest point in the history of American trade, unless possibly during the war, when entirely abnormal circumstances controlled prices. From these high prices there was a subsequent disastrous reaction and extensive failures. In the matter of the supply of tea, the total exports from China and India increased from 234,000,000 lbs. in 1873 to 337,000,000 lbs. in 1885, or 44 per cent. ; the exports from India having increased from 35,000,000 lbs. in 1879 to 68,000,000 lbs. in 1885.*

" Hops.—The report of the German Hop-growers' Association for 1886 estimates the quantity grown throughout the world in that year at 93,340 tons, and the annual consumption at only 83,200 tons ; so that there was an excess of production over consumption in 1886 of nearly 10,000 tons. As might have been expected, there was a notable decline in the world's prices for hops.

" Such having been the production and price experience in recent years of the world's great food commodities, attention is next invited to a similar record of experience in respect to the metals.

" Iron.—Sir Lowthian Bell, recognised as one of the best authorities on the production of iron and steel, in his testimony before the Royal Commission of 1885, fixed the world's production of pig-iron in 1870 at 11,565,000 tons, which increased to 14,345,000 tons in 1872. From that date production continued almost stationary until

---

* The present Chancellor of the Exchequer, Mr. Goschen, in his Budget speech for 1887, called attention to the following curious incident of financial disturbance growing out of a change in the quality of a staple commodity (tea), which, in turn, has been contingent on a change in the locality or country of its production : " Whereas, ten years ago," he said, " we received 156,000,000 lbs. of tea from China and 28,000,000 lbs. from India, or 184,000,000 lbs. altogether, in 1886 we received 145,000,000 lbs. from China and 81,000,000 lbs. from India. In the transfer of consumption of tea from the tea of China to that of India we have to put up with a loss of revenue, owing to the curious fact that the teas of India are stronger than the teas of China, and therefore go further ; so that a smaller quantity of tea is required to make the same number of cups of tea." Mr. Goschen further called attention to the fact that " the fall in the price of tea and sugar has been so great, that whereas in 1866 a pound of tea and a pound of sugar would have cost 2s. 6d., and in 1876, 2s. 1¼d., in 1886 they would have cost only 1s. 7¼d., or 3d. less than they would have cost in 1866 with all the duties taken off."

1879, when it was 14,048,000 tons. 'After 1879 an extraordinary change became apparent in the volume of the make, for during the ensuing five years the average make was 18,000,000 tons, and in 1883 it rose to 21,063,000 tons, or nearly 50 per cent. more than it was in 1879.' The witness further estimated that while the product of iron increased in the United Kingdom at the rate of 131 per cent. from 1870 to 1884, the increase in the production of the rest of the world during the same period had been 237 per cent.

" The tables of the American Iron and Steel Association, prepared by Mr. James M. Swank, indicate an increase in the pig-iron product of the world, from 1870 to 1886 inclusive, of about 100 per cent. All authorities are, therefore, substantially agreed that the increase in the production of this commodity in recent years has been not only far in excess of the increase of the world's population in general, but also of the increase of the population of the principal iron-producing countries. Thus, for example, in the United States the production increased from 4,044,526 gross tons in 1885 to 5,683,329 tons in 1886, an increase of 1,638,803 tons, or 40 per cent.

" Under such circumstances the prices of pig-iron throughout the world has rapidly declined, and in the case of some varieties touched in 1885-86 the lowest points in the history of the trade. American pig, which sold in February, 1880, for $45 per ton, declined almost continuously until September, 1885, when the low point of $16⅝ was reached; while in Great Britain, Cleveland pig, which sold for £4. 17s. 1d. in 1872, and £2. 5s. in 1880, declined to £1. 10s. 9d. in 1886. The decline in Bessemer steel rails in the English market was from £12. 1s. 1d. in 1874 to less than £4 in 1887. In the United States, Bessemer steel rails, which commanded $58 per ton at the mills in 1880, fell to $28·25 at the close of the year 1884, returning to $39½ in March, 1887.

" Reviewing specifically the causes which have contributed to the above-noted extraordinary decline in the prices of iron, the following points are worthy of notice :—

" *First.* The testimony of Sir Lowthian Bell shows that foreign countries have within recent years, and contrary to former experience, increased their production of iron in a far greater ratio than Great Britain, which was formerly the chief factor in the world's supply;

and in consequence have become formidable competitors with Great Britain not only in their own territories, but also in neutral markets. New fields of iron-ore have been discovered in Germany, France, and Belgium, very analogous in point of character to those which, by discovery and development, about the year 1850, in the north of England, led to the subsequent great and rapid increase of British iron production.

" *Second.* The power of producing iron with a given amount of labour and capital has in recent years greatly increased. For example, the average product per man of the furnaces of Great Britain, which for 1870 was estimated at 173 tons, is reported to have been 194 tons in 1880, and 261 tons in 1884.

" *Third.* The substitution of steel for iron has resulted in a notable diminution of the consumption of iron for attainment of a given result; or, in other words, more work is attainable from a less weight of material. Sir Lowthian Bell, in his testimony before the Royal Commission, stated that a ship of 1,700 tons requires 17 per cent. less in weight of pig-iron in being built of steel rather than of iron, and is capable of doing 7 per cent. more work.

" Again, the quantity of pig-iron requisite for keeping a railroad in repair will depend greatly upon the state in which iron enters into construction; rails of steel, for example, having a far greater durability than rails of iron.*

" A further example of recent economic disturbance consequent

---

* Opinions as yet vary greatly as to the comparative durability of iron and steel rails. In the testimony given before the Royal Commission of 1885, Mr. I. T. Smith, Manager of the Barrow Steel Company, gave it as his opinion that the life of a steel rail is three times that of an iron rail, adding: " My reason for saying so is, that I know that upon the London and North-Western Railway, where steel rails have been now in use more than twenty years, they consider it so."

Sir Lowthian Bell, also, in testifying before the Commission on the effect on the iron trade of Great Britain from the expected longer duration of steel rails, says: " Assuming iron rails to last twelve, and steel rails twenty-four years, instead of the railways now in existence in the United Kingdom requiring 465,648 tons annually for repairs, 232,824 tons will suffice for the purpose. Although this only involves the saving of a comparative small weight of pig-iron, it means less work for remelting and for our rolling-mills, say to the extent of 4,000 to 5,000 tons per week." The difference in duration of iron and steel rails is not, however, in itself a complete measure of the amount of pig-iron required for renewals. This arises from the fact that an iron rail splits up and becomes useless long before the actual wear, as measured by the diminution of weight, renders it unsafe, which often happens when the loss of weight does not exceed 4 per cent. of the original weight. Steel rails, on the other hand, go on losing weight until they are from 10 to 20 per cent. lighter than when they were laid down, before becoming unsafe.

upon changes in the manufacture of iron—characterised by the Secretary of the British Iron Trade Association in his Report for 1886 as ' one of the most remarkable of modern times '—is to be found in the rapid disuse of the system invented about one hundred years ago by Henry Cort for converting pig-iron into malleable iron by the so-called process of ' puddling.' Twenty years ago the use of this process was almost universal—to-day it is almost a thing that has passed; and the loss of British capital invested in puddling furnaces which have been abandoned in the ten years from 1875 to 1885 is estimated to have approximated £4,667,000, involving in Great Britain alone a displacement or transfer of workmen to other branches of industry during the same period of about 39,000.

" COPPER.—This metal touched the lowest price on record in 1886, Lake Superior copper in New York falling from 25 cents per pound in 1880 to $9\frac{1}{2}$ cents in August, 1886 ; and in the case of no other single commodity is the connection between the decline in price and the increase of production so well established and so significant. The increase in the copper product of the world is estimated by Mr. Sauerbeck to have been 97 per cent. in the thirteen years from 1873 to 1885 inclusive; while, according to the Report of the United States Geological Survey, 1886, the increase from 1879 to 1885 was nearly 47 per cent. (46·8). The countries which have most notably contributed to this increased product have been the United States and Spain and Portugal ; the increase in the case of the former having been from 23,000 tons in 1879 to 74,053 tons in 1885; and in that of the latter from 32,677 tons to 45,749 tons in the same period. As in all other like cases, the disturbing effect on the industries involved—mining and smelting—contingent on this rapid and remarkable fall in prices, was very great, and in all quarters of the world. In Montana, the Montana Copper Company, with an annual product of 8,000,000 lbs. of pure copper, entirely suspended operations ; and the Anaconda Company, with an annual product of 36,000,000 lbs., shut down twenty out of twenty-eight furnaces, and discharged most of its hands at the mine. In Chili, production during the year 1885 was diminished to the extent of about 10 per cent. In Germany, the great Mansfield mine, which reported gross profits in 1884 of 5,675,000 marks, sustained a loss in the operations of 1885 of 653,338 marks, and its managers have since sought relief by petitioning the Imperial Government for an imposition of a higher tariff on the imports of copper into the Empire. For the years 1881-83 the great San Domingo mine in Portugal paid annual dividends of 12½ per cent. ; in 1885 the annual rate was reduced to 3¾ per cent. It is important also to note, as throwing light upon the problem of the recent reduction of prices, that while in the case of copper the increase of product has been confessedly immense, three other agencies —one permanent and the other two of a temporary character—have contributed to its recent decline in price. The *first* is, that there has been a reduction in the cost of mining, smelting, and marketing copper at the principal mines of the world, owing to improved processes and reduced rates of transportation contingent on railroad construction. In the case of the Lake Superior mines this reduction is very striking; in the 'Quincy' mine, for example, the cost of production in cents per lb. having been reduced from 10·03 in 1881 to 7·50 in 1885, and in the 'Atlantic' from 13·80 to 9·37 in the corresponding period. *Second*, the recent discovery and rapid development of new and rich mines in Montana, Arizona, the Dominion of Canada, and elsewhere, have left a feeling of apprehension in the world's market as to the conditions of the supply of this metal in the future. *Third*, the consumption of copper in Europe for the year 1886 fell off 14,000 tons below the average for the two preceding years—a result attributed mainly to the dulness of the shipbuilding and the various metal industries.

" LEAD experienced a decline, comparing the highest market prices in New York in January, 1880 and 1885 respectively, of about 39 per cent. ; or, comparing the average prices for New York and London for the same years, about 30 per cent. The world's production of lead between the years 1880 and 1883 appears to have increased in nearly the same ratio, or far in excess of the increase of the world's population within the same period. With an approaching exhaustion of a number of the heaviest lead-producing mines in the Rocky Mountains,* and a notable decline in the lead product of British ores (50,328 tons in 1882, as compared with 37,687 tons in 1885), the price of lead tends to increase. The decline in the price of lead above noted occasioned the suspension or bankruptcy of many English lead-mining companies, and during the year 1885 much distress from this cause was

---

* Report of the United States Geological Survey, 1886.

reported as existing among English lead-miners. The following is an example of another economic disturbance contingent on changes in the production and price of lead: formerly the domestic supply in the United States of white lead, and of all paints the basis of which is oxide of lead, was derived almost exclusively from manufactories situated upon the Atlantic seaboard; but with the discovery and working of the so-called silver-lead mines of the States and Territories west of the Mississippi, and the production of large quantities of lead as a product residual or secondary to silver, the inducements offered for the manu-facture of white lead and lead-paints, through local reductions in the price of the raw material and the saving of freights, have been sufficient to almost destroy the former extensive white lead and paint business in the eastern sections of the United States, and transfer it to the western.

"NICKEL not many years ago was a scarce metal, of limited uses, and commanded comparatively high prices. Latterly, the discovery of new and cheaper sources of supply has tended to throw upon the market an amount in excess of the world's present average yearly consumption —estimated at between 800 and 900 tons—and as a consequence, there has been ' over-production, and unsatisfactory prices to dealers.' There is, moreover, little prospect that prices in respect to this metal will ever revive—one mine in New Caledonia alone being estimated as capable of producing two or three thousand tons annually, if required; while the discovery of richer and more abundant ore deposits than have ever before been known is reported as having resulted from the construction of the Canadian Pacific Railway.

" TIN.—The production and price experiences of this metal during the last quarter of a century have been very curious. The world's consumption of tin from 1860-64 constantly tended to be in excess of production, and prices rose from £87 (the lowest figure) in 1864 to £159 (the highest) in 1872. In this latter year the mines of Australia began to produce very largely, and in a short time afforded a supply equal to one-third of the world's current consumption. Under such circumstances the price of tin rapidly declined, and in October, 1878, touched £52. 10s., the lowest price ever known in history—a decline of 66 per cent. For some years past, however, the product of tin in Australia has been declining, that of the ' Straits' increasing, and that of England and other countries remaining nearly stationary; but the consumption of tin throughout the world has gone on continuously increasing, until now the surplus stock is being so rapidly reduced, that unless new sources of supply are developed famine rates may again occur, prices having advanced continuously from £52. 10s. in 1879 to £107 in June, 1887.

"Tin-Plates.—Owing to a well-recognised tendency of consumption to exceed production, tin-plates, in common with tin, ruled at what were termed 'famine' prices in 1872, and for some years previous, the average price for 'coke' plates being from 26s. to 27s. per ton. Since 1872 the decline has been in excess of 50 per cent.—the quotation for the first half of the year 1887 having been from 12s. 6d. to 13s. per box. This remarkable and steady decline in the prices of this commodity during the last fifteen years is as clearly and certainly understood as in the case of tin above noticed, and is referable to three causes : *First*, the reduction in the cost of the metal tin ; *second*, to the revolution in the manufacture of iron, and the extensive substitution of steel (plates) in place of charcoal and puddled iron plates ; *third*, to new processes of manufacture and tinning, a modern tin-plate mill turning out every twenty-four hours more than double the product of old-fashioned mills, without any increase in expenditure for motive power or labour. Supply and consumption alike, under such circumstances, have increased to an enormous extent, and the tin-plate trade, instead of being a minor industry of the world, as was formerly and not remotely the case, has become one of great magnitude. The decline in prices has, however, brought nothing of prosperity to the British tin-plate manufacturing industry ; as out of an average of eighty-two works in existence during recent years in South Wales, there have been no less than forty failures.*

" Quicksilver.—Excepting petroleum and quinine, the decline in price of this metal seems to have been greater in recent years than that

---

* An attempt on the part of Germany to break in upon the almost complete monopoly of the manufacture of tin-plates enjoyed by Great Britain, by imposing a heavy duty on their importation, has been singularly unsuccessful, domestic (German) production and exports having diminished, and exports increased, as will appear from the following table :—

Year.					Production. Tons.	Imports. Tons.	Exports. Tons.
1885 ..	..	..	..	..	4,892	5,798	186
1878 ..	..	..	..	..	8,582	5,307	1,696

of any other leading commodity—*i.e.*, from £26 per flask (the highest) on the London market, in 1874, to £5. 2s. 6d. (lowest) in 1884 ; and from $118 (highest) to $26 (lowest) on the San Francisco market during the same period; a decline of 77·1 per cent. The explanation of this movement of price is to be found mainly in the circumstance that California, which furnishes nearly one-half of the world's supply of this metal, increased her production from 30,077 flasks in 1870 to 79,684 flasks in 1877 ; and although, as the result of low prices, only ten of thirty working mines of California were in operation in 1885 (none of which paid a dividend in that year), the generally increased supply of quicksilver, coupled with its diminished use in the reduction of silver ores—consequent on the introduction and use of cheaper processes—has thus far prevented any material augmentation in its price, the London quotation for June, 1887, having been £6. 15s. per flask.

" SILVER.—The annual supply of silver from the mines of the world has largely increased since 1872-73, the period covered by the marked decline in the market price of silver ; or, according to the estimates of the Bureau of the Mint of the United States, from $65,000,000 in 1872 to $102,168,000 in 1881; $114,000,000 in 1883, and $124,000,000 in 1885, an increase in supply in fourteen years of 90·7 per cent.

" COAL.—The decline in the export prices of British coal, comparing the average for 1867-77 with 1886, was about 33 per cent. The decline in the average annual price of anthracite coal (by the cargo at Philadelphia), comparing 1870 with 1880, was 38 per cent., but as between 1870 and 1886 it was only 6·6 per cent. The total production of all kinds of coal in the United States in 1886, according to the returns of the United States Geological Survey, shows a net gain of 1,785,000 short tons, as compared with 1885, but a loss in value at the point of production of $4,419,420.

" The increase in the product of the five chief coal-producing countries in the world—Great Britain, the United States, Germany, France, and Belgium—from 1870 to 1886 inclusive, has been in excess of 80 per cent.; Great Britain increasing her product from 109,000,000 tons in 1870 to 159,351,000 in 1885 ; and the United States from 38,468,000 in 1870 to 112,743,000 short tons in 1886. On the other hand, the amount of coal displaced from use in the United States in 1886 by the introduction and use of natural gas is estimated by the United

States Geological Survey at 6,353,000 tons, valued at $9,847,000. In Germany the increase reported was from 36,041,000 tons in 1873 to 55,000,000 tons in 1883. In 1870 the average output of coal per miner in the British coal mines—counting in all the men employed—was 250 tons, an amount never before reached. In 1879 this average had increased to 280 tons per man, and in 1884 the average for the five preceding years was reported at 322 tons, an increase of 42 gross tons of 21 cwts. per man per annum. For Germany the increase was from 261 tons in 1881 to 269 tons in 1883; and in Belgium, for corresponding years, from 165 tons to 178 tons per miner.

" Recent inventions have also done much to reduce the amount of coal formerly used to effect industrial results, particularly in the case of blast-furnaces and coke-ovens. For example, at blast-furnaces coal was formerly used for heating the boilers that furnished steam for blowing, hoisting, &c., and for heating the air which was blown into the stacks. Now, a well-ordered set of blast-furnaces does not use a single ounce of coal, except what goes in to melt the ore. The whole of the heat used to produce the steam required in connection with the furnace and for heating the stoves for making the hot-blast is obtained from the gases which rise to the top of the stacks in the process of smelting the iron, and which formerly was all thrown away.

" Petroleum.—Crude petroleum declined in the American market from an average of $3·86 (gold) per barrel in 1870 to $87\frac{1}{2}$ cents per barrel in 1885 and $71\frac{1}{2}$ cents in 1886, a total decline of over 80 per cent.

" The American annual production (including Canada) increased during the same period from 5,510,745 barrels in 1870 to 30,626,100 barrels in 1882, declining to 25,798,000 barrels in 1886.

" That the production and price experiences of the great staple fibres of commerce and consumption in recent years have not been dissimilar to those of the foods and metals will also appear from the following :—

" Cotton.—Comparing 1860 with 1885, the decline in the price of American cotton (middling uplands) in the New York market has not been material. The year 1886, however, witnessed a decline to a lower point ($8\frac{13}{16}$) than has been reached, with one exception, since the year 1855, the exception occurring just after the failure of the Glasgow

Bank in Scotland, in 1878, the lowest quotations in both years being exactly the same. On the other hand, the increase in the world's supply of cotton in recent years has been very considerable, the American crop increasing from 3,930,000 bales in 1872-73 to 6,575,000 bales in 1885-86, or 67 per cent. ; while the supply of the world for the corresponding period is estimated to have increased from 6,524,000 bales to 8,678,000 bales, or at the rate of about 32 per cent. Such an increase in production would undoubtedly have occasioned a more marked decline in price had it not been for a great and coincident increase in the world's consumption of cotton fabrics, which, in turn, was undoubtedly in consequence of a material decline in the cost of the same, as the result of improvements in machinery and methods of production ; the equivalent of the labour of an operative in the factories of New England having increased from 12,164 yards in 1850 to 19,293 in 1870, and 28,032 in 1884 ; while the reduction in the price of standard sheetings from 1850 to 1885 has been about 10 per cent., and of standard prints and printing-cloths during the same period approximately 40 per cent.

" WOOL.—According to the statistics of Mr. Sauerbeck (*Journal of Statistical Society*, March, 1887), the price of merino wool (Port Philip, Australia, average fleece), comparing the averages of the series of years 1867-77 and 1878-85, declined 10·7 per cent. ; or, comparing the average price of 1867-77 with that of the single year 1886, when wool 'was cheaper than at any time within the memory of the present generation,' 27 per cent. Certain fibres classed with wool, and known as 'alpaca' and 'mohair,' and the grade of long-combing English wools known as 'Lincoln,' experienced a much greater decline after 1874-75, owing to the curious circumstance that a change in fashion in those years almost entirely and suddenly destroyed any demand for the before popular, stiff, lustrous fabrics manufactured from such wools for female wear, and substituted in their place the soft and pliable cloths that are made from merino wools.

" The increase in the production and world's supply of raw wools, from the years 1860 to 1885 inclusive, was about 100 per cent. According to Mr. Sauerbeck's tables, the increase from 1873 to 1885 inclusive was 20 per cent. ; according to Messrs. Helmuth Schwartze & Co., of London, the increase from 1871-75 to 1881-85 was 23 per cent. ; and from 1871-75 to 1886, 35 per cent. The wool-clip of the United States increased from 264,000,000 lbs. in 1880 to 329,000,000 lbs. in 1885, or 24·6 per cent. in six years. Such an increase in the world's supply of wool would undoubtedly have resulted in a greater decline in prices had not the increase been accompanied, as was the case with cotton, with a very marked increase during the last quarter of a century in the world's consumption—*i.e.*, from 2·03 lbs. of clean wool per head in 1860 to 2·66 lbs. in 1886.

" SILK.—The decline in the price of silk (Tsatlee), according to Mr. Sauerbeck, from the average price of 1867-77 to the average of 1886, was about 40 per cent. ; and the average increase in supply of all varieties of silk-fibre, comparing 1873 with 1885, was reported by the same authority as about 12 per cent. No relation between the price movements of this commodity and supply and demand, or any other agencies, can, however, be established which fails to take into account the great increase in the use of ramie and other fibres and materials, within recent years, as substitutes for or adulterations of silk in the manufacture of fabrics, and which must obviously have an effect on the price of raw silk equivalent to an increase in its supply.

" JUTE.—Good medium jute declined in the London market from £17 per ton in 1874 to an average of £11. 10s. in 1886, or more than 32 per cent. The increase in exports from British India was from 5,206,570 cwts. in 1876 to 10,348,909 cwts. in 1883, or 98 per cent.

" NITRATE OF SODA.—The recent price experiences of nitrate of soda (Chilian saltpetre) have been very curious. The supply of this article, which corresponds to the more valuable nitrate of potash (true saltpetre), is practically limited to one locality on the earth's surface —a rainless, desert tract—in the province of Tarapacá, which formerly belonged to Peru, but has recently been annexed to Chili. It is cheaply and plentifully obtained, at points from fifty to ninety miles from the coast, by dissolving out the nitrate salt from the desert earth, which it impregnates, with water, and concentrating the solution by boiling to the point where the nitrate separates by crystallisation. Up to the year 1845 it was an article so little known to commerce that only 6,000 tons were annually exported ; but as its value as a fertilising agent in agriculture, and as a cheap source of nitrogen in the manufacture of nitric acid, became recognised, the demand for it rapidly increased, until the amount exported in 1883 was estimated at 570,000 tons, or more than a thousand million pounds. To meet this demand and obtain the profit resulting from substituting skilful for primitive methods of extracting and marketing the nitrate, foreign capital, mainly English, extensively engaged in the business. A large amount of English-made machinery, and many English engineers and mechanics, were sent out and planted in the desert ; additional supplies of water were secured, and a railroad fifty-nine miles in length constructed to the port of Iquique on the sea-coast, for the transportation of coal, provisions, and other material *up*, and the nitrate as a return freight *down*. So energetically, moreover, was the work pressed, that at the last a most complete establishment — constructed under English auspices, the business employing, when in full operation, six hundred men—was prosecuted unremittingly, by night (by the agency of the electric light) as well as by day. The result was exactly what might have been anticipated. The export of nitrate, which was 319,000 tons in 1881, rose to 570,000 tons in 1883 ; and prices at the close of 1883 declined with great rapidity, to the extent of more than 50 per cent., or to a point claimed to be below the cost of production. Such a result, threatening the whole business with disaster, led to an agreement on the part of all the interests concerned to limit from June, 1884, to January, 1887, the product of every establishment to 25 per cent. of its capacity. But, notwithstanding these well-devised measures, prices have not been restored to their former figures, the average price per cwt. in London having been 10s. in 1886, as compared with an average of 14s. for 1867-77. For May, 1887, the quotations had advanced to 11s. and 11s. 5d. This case is especially worthy of notice, because it constitutes another example of a great and rapid decline in the price of a standard and valuable commodity in the world's commerce, and for which—all the facts being clearly understood —it is not possible to assign any other cause than that of production in excess of any current demand for consumption, and which in turn has been solely contingent on the employment, under novel conditions, of improved methods for overcoming territorial and climatic difficulties.

" Concurrently with the fall in the price of nitrate of soda, saltpetre, or nitrate of potash, also notably declined from 28s. 3d. in 1880 to 21s. in 1887 (for English refined), a fact which seems to find a sufficient explanation in the circumstance that nitrate of soda can be used to a certain extent as a substitute for nitrate of potash, and that the export of the latter from India, the country of chief supply, increased from 352,995 cwts. in 1881 to 451,917 cwts. in 1885, or 36 per cent.

" PAPER.—A quarter of a century ago, or less, paper was made almost exclusively from the fibres of cotton and linen rags; and, with an enormous and continually increasing demand, paper and rags not only rapidly increased in price, but continually tended to increase, and thus greatly stimulated effort for the discovery and utilisation of new fibrous materials for the manufacture of paper. These efforts have been so eminently successful, that immense quantities of pulp suitable for the manufacture of paper are now made from the fibres of wood, straw, and various grasses, and so cheaply, that the prices of fair qualities of book-paper have declined since the year 1872 to the extent of fully 50 per cent., while in the case of ordinary 'news' the decline has been even greater. Rags, although still extensively used, have, by the competitive supply of substitute materials, and a consequent comparative lack of demand, been also greatly cheapened.

" QUININE.—But in no one article has the decline in recent years been more extraordinary and thoroughly capable of explanation than in the case of sulphate of quinine, a standard chemical preparation, used extensively all over the world for medicinal purposes. In 1865 the highest price of sulphate of quinine in the English market was 4s. 4d. per ounce, which gradually advanced to 9s. 6d. in 1873, receding to 6s. 9d. in 1876. In the subsequent year, owing to an interruption in the exportation of cinchona-bark from South America by civil war in New Granada, and by low water in the Magdalena River, the price advanced to the unprecedentedly high figure of 16s. 6d. per ounce, receding to 13s. in 1879 and 12s. in 1880. In 1883, identically the same article sold in Europe for 3s. 6d. per ounce, and in 1885 for 2s. 6d., a result entirely attributable to the successful and extensive introduction and growth of the cinchona-tree in the British and Dutch East Indies, and to the further very curious circumstance, that while the cinchona-barks from South America—the product of indigenous trees—yield on an average not over 2 per cent. of quinine, the bark of the cultivated tree in Java is reported to yield 8 to 12 per cent.

" The decline in the prices of many chemicals, due to improvements in methods and to excess of production, has also been very great— the decline in soda-ash from 1872 having been 54 per cent., while bleaching powders (chloride of lime) declined from £10 in 1873 to £6. 15s. in 1878, receding to £9 in 1887.

" Many other commodities, of greater or less importance, might be included in this investigation, with a deduction of like results; but this is not necessary, for it is difficult to see how anyone can rise from an examination of the record of the production and price experiences of the commodities which have been specified—which, it must be remembered, represent, considered either from the standpoint of qualities or values, the great bulk of the trade, commerce, and consumption of the world— without being abundantly and conclusively satisfied that the decline in their prices which has occurred during the last ten or fifteen years, or from 1873, has been so largely due to conditions affecting their supply and demand, that if any or all other causes whatever have contributed to such a result, the influence exerted has not been appreciable ; and further, that if the prices of all other commodities not included in the above record had confessedly been influenced by a scarcity of gold, the claims preferred by the advocates of the latter theory could not be fairly entitled to any more favourable verdict than that of ' not proven.' "

In his letter to *The Times* of September 11th, 1887, Mr. Daniel Watney took a right view of the currency question then under discussion in reference to Indian trade, when he wrote as follows:—" It would be a pity to blame the currency question as though it acted in some mysterious way as a protection to Indian industry, when the cause is simply a natural development, which has reached during the last 12 years, I believe, an increase of 57 per cent., and which ought to be hailed with the liveliest satisfaction by every patriotic Englishman."

CHAPTER VI.

VIEWS UPON THE CURRENCY AND KINDRED QUESTIONS OF CONTEMPORARY WRITERS.

DURING the progress of the bi-metallic movement unsound views found favour in many quarters where the Tory line had more or less to be adopted. One of the threads of this line was Fair Trade, and it was generally to be found advocated by people professing the Conservative creed. It is always satisfactory to find an organ of that party admitting, perhaps inadvertently, into its columns facts which very seriously undermine the arguments of Fair Traders and Protectionists. *The St. James's Gazette* of January 12th, 1888, did this when it summarised a Blue-Book on " Wages in the Past Half-Century," issued by the Commercial Department of the Board of Trade. The following is the summary, which we take as an accurate condensation of the facts. This paper disposes to a large extent of the complaints and lamentations poured out by M. Emile de Laveleye, to which we refer elsewhere.

" WAGES IN THE PAST HALF-CENTURY.

" One of the most valuable publications ever issued by a Government Department has just been issued by the Commercial Department of the Board of Trade. It consists of nearly 450 pages of tables, collected from returns and statements relating to wages which have appeared in Parliamentary papers for the last fifty years or more. Here at length we have the most authentic data for deciding the much-discussed question whether the earnings of the working classes have risen or fallen during the past half-century. Whatever the truth may be, it lies hidden in this mass of figures ; and we may be sure that statisticians, economists, and politicians will eagerly seek to discover it. Of course the task is far from easy. The first difficulty is to reduce the returns to a common basis. The rate of wages is given variously for the day, the week, the month, and even the year ; the hours of labour are sometimes stated and sometimes not, and the classification of trades is by no means uniform. To work out precise comparisons would, therefore, be a most laborious task, though the result would be well worth the pains. We shall content ourselves with one or two examples roughly selected.

" Take the Manchester cotton trade to begin with. In 1810 fine spinners earned 42s. 6d. per week ; four years later this had dropped to 32s. ; and in 1832 the wages were as low as from 20s. to 25s. At this figure they remained for a good many years ; but in 1874 we find them up to 42s. and even 50s. ; in 1877 they ranged from 29s. 8d. to 55s., according to the class of work and the number of spindles, and then in 1883 we have a drop to 31s. These fluctuations are characteristic of a good many trades : high wages in the early years of the century, then a decided decrease, then (about 1874-79) a substantial recovery, and finally, a fair average rate, midway between the great inflations and depressions of former years. Colliers' wages fell from 21s. to 13s. in South Wales during 1840-44 ; rose to 36s. in 1877, and fell again to 26s. in 1883. Iron-rollers earned as much as 69s. per week in 1840, but only 45s. in 1845 ; this sum had fallen in 1849 to 35s. 6d. ; then in 1877 we find a recovery to 42s. 6d. ; and in the last return the rate is stated as 55s. The general rule thus established by three of the chief industries of the country holds good in regard to the great majority of the smaller trades ; and it is gratifying to find that the tendency now is an upward one, although the general rate of wages may never again reach the abnormal height of ten or twelve years ago.

" For practical purposes the last two or three decades are the most profitable to study. That, on the whole, wages *are higher now than they were during the period which immediately followed the introduction of steam and of manufacturing machinery may be taken as proved.* The question which interests us at this moment is, whether they have advanced or decreased during the modern industrial period in which the conditions of production and consumption have not materially altered. In the cotton trade there was during the years 1839 to 1859 an average advance in wages of from 10 to 25 per cent. From 1859 to 1875 the advance (after an intermediate depression) averaged a further 25 per cent. By 1877 a fall of about 10 or 15 per cent. had taken place; in 1880 we find a slight rise, and this was fully maintained in 1883, when wages were quite 30 per cent. above the rate of twenty years earlier. These results are calculated on the Manchester rates. To deal with those given for Glasgow, Bristol, and other places would take us too far into details; and, besides, any comparison on the basis of locality would be fallacious, except in the case of the chief seat of a trade, seeing that, although twenty or thirty years ago wages in identical trades varied greatly in different parts, the action of trade unions has since tended to equalise them throughout the country. In the calico printing and dyeing trade, there has been a marked increase in the wages of the sketch-makers, die-cutters, and machine-engravers; but in the less skilled departments of labour—the machine-hands, colour-mixers, &c.— it has been somewhat slight. In the flax manufacture the past twenty years have brought an increase of more than 15 per cent. in the rate of wages. In Belfast, power-weavers were earning from 1s. to 1s. 3d. a day in 1857; they now earn 1s. 10d., working only fifty-six hours a week instead of sixty. In the woollen trade, the wages of sorters have been— 21s. in 1839, 22s. 6d. in 1859, 22s. to 32s. in 1866, 28s. in 1874, 24s. in 1880, and 25s. in 1883; and, with few exceptions, similar fluctuations have taken place in the wages of other woollen mill-hands. As a rule, the wages in the wool trade have been higher in the south of England and in Scotland than in Yorkshire and Lancashire; but (as in the linen trade also) they have been lowest in Ireland. It will surprise no one to hear that wages in the silk trade have steadily fallen. Men who are now glad to get 19s. a week would have found plenty of employment at 36s. twenty years ago. On the other hand, first-class lace-makers have advanced from 35s. in 1866 to from £3 to

£5 in 1883; a truly astonishing increase, due, if we mistake not, to improved technical knowledge. Even curtain-hands can earn from 70s. to 80s. on piece-work.

"Leaving the textile trades, we come to coal and ironstone mining. In these industries the wages are calculated on the output, and a skilful workman can always earn a great deal more than a bungler. The average wage in the Midland district in 1860 was 22s. 6d.; in 1883 it was 25s. 9d. Colliers' wages touched their highest point in 1867-8, when a good hewer could make £2 a week. Wages in the iron and steel manufactures followed pretty much the same course as in coal and iron mining. Puddlers in 1866 could earn from 7s. 6d. to 7s. 10d. a day; in 1877 only 5s. 7d.; and in 1883, 5s. 10d. Iron-moulders have maintained a steady rate of 6s. for many years, though in some places they have gone down as low as 5s.—notably at Newcastle in 1867-8. *In the manufacture of machinery there has been a gratifying increase since* 1880, when men who now earn from 33s. to 37s. per week earned only 30s. As for ship-building, the transition from wood to iron and steel, and the migration of the trade from the Thames, the Severn, and the Mersey to the Tees, the Tyne, and the Clyde, can be clearly traced. On the Clyde fitters earned 27s. per week in 1863, 28s. 9d. in 1866, 30s. 6d. in 1880, and 33s. to 36s. (day work), or 42s. to 67s. (piece-work) in 1883. Since then there have been, to our knowledge, some reductions, but they are not shown in these returns.

"We must pass over the pottery, glass, leather, chemical, sugar, paper, printing, brewing, building, and other trades, in order to come at once to an industry which cannot be overlooked—agriculture. The returns here are extremely full and precise, though they only go back to 1860, and only come down to 1870. The wages of men, women, and children are stated as at the end of each of three quarters of the year, and for each county in England and Wales. Returns are also given for Scotland and Ireland. One fact, at any rate, is clear at the first glance: *there has been a considerable and general increase. The highest rates recorded for* 1860 *become the normal rates in* 1870, *and in many instances are exceeded. In some counties the increase has been as much as* 80 *per cent. With this most gratifying fact we leave the subject for the present.*"

The following appears in *Bradstreet's* of October 23rd, 1886:—

" MR. MORETON FREWEN AND THE SILVER QUESTION.

" Mr. Moreton Frewen has written to *Bradstreet's*, arguing that the persistent fall in the price of American wheat is really due to the fluctuations in Indian exchange and the decline in the gold value of the silver rupee. Referring to the evidence laid before the British Royal Trade Commission, Mr. Frewen says:—

" Mr. Palgrave, the ex-editor of the London *Economist*, says: ' Speaking generally, every fluctuation of 1d. in the rate of exchange is equivalent to an alteration of 17d. per quarter in the selling price of wheat in England.' That is to say, the fall from 22d. to 16d. in the value of the rupee has reduced the Mark Lane price of wheat by more than 1s. a bushel, and has marked down the price of every bushel of wheat grown on this continent 25c. The evidence received by the Commission all pointed in one direction. Owing to the demonetisation and suspension of coinage, silver is losing its exchange value in terms of gold, but is not losing its value at home in the myriad-peopled East. And if this is the case, and the evidence is most positive and conclusive, then the present depression of prices for your agricultural exports is abundantly accounted for.

" The above illustrates how men of Mr. Frewen's views are prone to ground arguments for serious political action on the surface facts of a given situation. Here is an attempt to trace a great movement in commerce to changes in the price of one of the articles constituting the tool of commerce—money. What is this movement in commerce? Nothing less than an increase in the railway facilities of India from 6,705 miles in 1875 to 12,005 miles in 1884-5; along with this the export of Indian wheat has developed from 10,429,000 bushels in

1876-77 to 39,313,000 bushels in 1885-86, the latter being the highest yearly export yet recorded. Here are the primary facts with respect to the recent course of India's foreign trade. Back of these is the fact of the great stimulus given to the production of wheat throughout the world by the short crops of Europe just previous to 1879. Wheat-growing in the United States received an immense stimulus. More wheat compelled cheaper prices, and low prices, in turn, tend to bring about increased consumption.

" Having regard to these great underlying facts, it would be far more reasonable to conclude that the fluctuations in the value of the rupee have been consequent thereon than the contrary. Yet this conclusion need not be set opposite the fallacies of Mr. Frewen. To an extent it may be true that the price of wheat at London is affected by the fluctuations in Indian exchange, and that the price in the United States is in turn affected. It is also true that when more rupees can be had for Indian wheat, the seeming effect, in the first instance, is to stimulate shipments. But only in the first instance. Just here is the weak point of Mr. Frewen's case. He assumes that the rupee is 'not losing its value at home in the myriad-peopled East.' As to the assumed point, facts are needed for light. In the first place, it is hardly reasonable to suppose the influences making for the serious decline in the price of silver, if not already, will in good time be fully felt wherever silver is used as a medium of exchange. But testimony as to the actual facts is not wanting. These, as must necessarily have been true, go to prove marked price reductions in India.

Mr. J. E. O'Conor, a statistician immediately familiar with Indian affairs, has undertaken to analyse the course of Indian exchanges and prices. Regarding the course of prices, Mr. O'Conor's position was set forth as follows in the letter of a London correspondent published in *Bradstreet's* of September 25th :—

" To sum up the case roughly, Mr. O'Conor shows that prices have fallen in India, say, 10 per cent. all round, and that therefore the Indian producer has not gained. On the other hand, exchange has fallen by 20 per cent., which is a gain to the exporter; but against this must be set a decline of about 30 per cent. in the gold prices obtained for the exported product in the consuming markets. The exporter, therefore, buys his goods 10 per cent. cheaper, but sells them at 30 per cent. lower prices, thus making a loss of 20 per cent., which is about made up to him by the decline in exchange. By this showing, then, the fall in silver, to which the decline in exchange is due, has benefited neither the producer nor exporter, and cannot, therefore, have stimulated the export trade. On the other hand, the loss to the Indian Government on its remittances has been very large.

" It is thus seen that the point assumed by Mr. Frewen is clearly in dispute with both the facts and the reasoning against his position.

" The readiness of Mr. Frewen, and others like him, to attribute the increased Indian wheat movement to fluctuations in the price of exchange is of a part with the arguments of those who find in the actions of Government a sufficient reason for the fall in silver. They persistently refuse to make due allowance for the tremendous results in improved means of transportation which the locomotive and its belongings have brought about."

One of the arguments of the bi-metallists has always been that the business of the country was going to ruin owing to their views not being adopted. Their great cry has always been: " Look at the existing depression in trade!" What are the hard facts of the case? We will quote from the statistics prepared in January, 1885, by the late Professor Leone Levi for Sir Arthur Bass, M.P., before the recovery in general business had unmistakably manifested itself. In that report he says:—

" Since 1867 the population has increased from about 30,000,000 to 36,000,000, and many vicissitudes have occurred in the rates of wages. After a period of unexampled prosperity in trade, the nation has experienced all the bitter fruit of a protracted depression; the relations between capital and labour have been frequently strained; and an important conference is about to be held for the purpose of considering whether the present system, whereby the products of industry are distributed between the various persons and classes of the community, is satisfactory, or, if not, by what means that system can be improved. It is under these circumstances that you have desired me to renew the inquiry into the amount of earnings of the labouring classes, and I have much pleasure in laying before you the results of my investigations.

" SECTION I.—NUMBER OF EARNERS.

" I have taken the number of earners in the different industries from the latest census, taking for my calculation only those under sixty-five years of age. In 1867 I found the number of workers to be 11,018,000; in 1881 they were 12,200,000. Assuming the working classes to comprise 70 per cent. of the population, and with small farmers, crofters, and others to number 26,000,000 persons, or 5,600,000 families, the 12,200,000 workers give 2·17 earners for every family.

" SECTION II.—WAGES.

" In most cases adult wages commence with the age of majority; but in the case of domestic servants, factory labourers, and others, persons of fifteen years and upwards usually earn full wages. In the case of domestic servants, seamen, and others, the value of board and lodging must be added to the money wages. So must the value of all allotments of land to agricultural labourers, and so the value of uniforms, liveries or other perquisites, wherever given.

" Section III.—Earners and Earnings.

" The number of earners and the amount of their earnings in 1867 and 1884 may be taken as follows :—

Occupations.	Number of Earners.		Amount of Earnings.		Average Earnings.	
	1884.	1867.	1884.	1867.	1884.	1867.
			£	£	£	£
Professional	400,000	300,000	16,000,000	10,000,000	40	33
Domestic	2,400,000	1,700,000	96,000,000	59,000,000	40	35
Commercial	900,000	700,000	45,000,000	39,000,000	60	55·14
Agricultural	1,900,000	2,700,000	57,000,000	84,000,000	34·14	31·2
Industrial	6,600,000	5,600,000	307,000,000	226,000,000	46·10	40
	12,200,000	11,000,000	521,000,000	418,000,000	42·14	38

" Thus, with an increase of less than 11 per cent. in the number of earners, there has been an increase of 24·64 per cent. in the amount of earnings, the average earning per head having increased from £38 in 1867 to £42. 14s. in 1884, or in the proportion of 12·37 per cent.

" Dividing the earners and earnings by age and sex, the results are as follows :—

Occupations.	Number of Earners.		Amount of Earnings.		Average Earnings.	
	1884.	1867.	1884.	1867.	1884.	1867.
			£	£	£	£
Males under 20........	1,650,000	1,200,000	29,000,000	23,000,000	18	19
Males, 20 and under 65..	6,530,000	5,900,000	363,000,000	293,000,000	57·2	51·7
Females under 20	1,300,000	1,300,000	30,000,000	27,000,000	22·17	20·15
Females, 20 and under 65	2,720,000	2,600,000	99,000,000	75,000,000	33	28·17
	12,200,000	11,000,000	521,000,000	418,000,000	43·10	38

" The total earnings thus calculated include the value of board and lodging wherever given. Deducting this item, the amount of money earnings may be estimated at £470,000,000."

We there read what every political economist and man of business with any penetrative insight into the

course of events can discover for himself, if he will quit
the limit of the little circle within which his prejudices
are confined, that "after a period of unexampled prosperity in trade, the nation has experienced all the bitter
fruit of a protracted depression." No quack doctoring
in the form of bi-metallism is of any use in such circumstances. You might as well invoke the aid of the deities
to arrest the violence of the tempest, which is the result
of natural disturbances, and which is necessary to
readjust a balance which in the course of nature has
been temporarily upset.

The following appeared in *The Pall Mall Gazette* of
August 26th, 1886 :—

"THE CASE FOR BI-METALLISM.

"BY M. EMILE DE LAVELEYE.

" Among the various causes of the present economic
crisis some are closely connected with the very progress
of civilisation; but there is certainly one which is solely
attributable to ill-judged legislation. I refer to the
proscription of silver. This metal, which from the
remotest antiquity was the universal monetary circulating medium, has been suddenly rejected by the mints
of all countries, India alone excepted. The business
transactions of the world were accomplished by means
of two-wheeled chariots, one wheel being of white metal
and the other of yellow. There has been a general
agreement to break one of these wheels, and yet people
seem surprised that the commerce of the world should
be so considerably affected !

" Who can fail to observe the sad results of the
fall in prices ? They are, alas ! but too clearly visible.

Great lowering of rent, and consequent reduction in expenditure of farmers and landlords, resulting in loss to all industries which supply the wants of these two important classes of consumers; cultivators losing money and clamouring for State intervention and agrarian measures—does not this, indeed, resume the Irish question? Holders of mortgaged estates almost ruined; for in many instances the property itself is no longer worth the mortgage upon it;* railway receipts on the decline, a most decisive proof of the stagnation of business; commercial and business men losing in nearly all their transactions, because the price of goods continues falling lower and lower; capital, meeting only with deceptions in all trading enterprises, withdrawing itself into such safe investments as Consols and the like; the initiative spirit dying, if not already dead, for who would dare to start any fresh enterprise when he sees nothing but ruin on all sides?

" It might be thought that this general fall in the price of provisions would be a benefit to the labourer and artisan; but of what avail is this if wages fall proportionately, and more especially if employment becomes scarce? Nothing is more cruel than a protracted period of depression of prices. One hears incessantly of failures,† suicides, strikes,‡ riots, and disturbances of all kinds. This is quite explicable. Coinage is the blood of the social body. A disturbance in the monetary

---

* See article, *St. James's Gazette*, on Mortgages.

† Never was there such a small number of commercial failures as since the fall in prices.

‡ Strikes have been almost unknown in this country of last years

circulation is at best a very serious disease, and it may prove fatal. I think none will deny that the production of gold is very inferior to the requirements of the world. Here are some statistics which clearly show this. The annual production is £18,000,000 ; the consumption for industries, which is ever on the increase, is £12,000,000; the average annual export to India (1881-1884) is £4,728,342 ; the losses, wear and tear amount to about a million – total, £17,000,000. There remains, therefore, just one million sterling yearly for the monetary requirements of the entire world, India excepted. Who dare maintain that this is sufficient? The gold-producing countries, such as America, Australia, and Russia, are precisely those whose inhabited territory and population are the most rapidly on the increase. They therefore retain more and more of the gold they produce for themselves. The quantity of gold sent by Australia to England is yearly diminishing; and as for America, not only she no longer sends us any, but she yearly withdraws a portion from Europe. Between 1875 and 1884 the imports of gold to the United States exceeded the exports by £25,000,000. After the suspension of the Bland Act the exports of gold to America will probably increase four or five millions sterling annually. What will then become of the European circulation? Even now—and the fact is without example in economic history—coinage is very nearly suspended in our Western world. France, Belgium, and Holland have coined nothing for the last six or seven years. All the fine machinery set up in the mints is lying idle. In England some few millions have been struck, but almost entirely from old sovereigns and half-sovereigns re-melted. Between 1879 and 1884 England only coined altogether £792,283, and during the same period Australia coined £24,112,000, and America \$381,955,000, or about £75,000,000—that is to say, £30,000,000 more than its total production of gold. The monetary stock in England is rapidly diminishing. In 1877 Bagehot estimated that she required an annual excess of importation of gold of four millions sterling; and in point of fact, between 1858 and 1875 this excess rose, on an average, to £4,432,000 annually. Between 1877 and 1884, according to Bagehot's calculation, England ought to have received an excess of £24,000,000. Instead of this, her circulation lost £7,940,408 exported, and £16,000,000 absorbed in arts; making together £23,940,408. The difference is therefore about 48 millions sterling.

" But it is argued gold is not lacking; it exists in superabundance, as quantities of it are lying idle in banks. It suffices to recall the most elementary principle of economic science to understand at once that monetary contraction never makes itself manifest by an absolute lack of gold, save in countries absolutely drained of the metal—as is, indeed, already the case in certain States. As the supply of gold diminishes, *cæteris paribus*, prices fall in proportion, and consequently less gold is necessary for effecting the same number of exchanges. If you do away with silver, gold will alone fulfil the same functions as previously the two metals conjointly, the buying power of the remaining coin having increased proportionately to the fall in prices; and as, on the other hand, this fall in prices is productive of an intense crisis and of general stagnation in business, commercial transactions generally are restricted, and gold, being unemployed, accumulates in banks. This is exactly what is now taking place. For instance, the reserve in the Bank of England is very small, and yet the rate of discount is low, there being so few demands. If you were to reduce the monetary stock to one-half what it is at present, the disturbance produced would be so violent, that the remaining gold would find no employment whatever; the less gold there is the more it will appear superabundant, for the less there is the less it is required. In prohibiting silver, lawgivers have violated both Nature's and History's laws; for Nature had placed at mankind's disposal two metals specially suitable as means of exchange, gold and silver, and History teaches us that civilised communities have always used them together.

"At the Paris Conference of 1878, Mr. Goschen predicted the disastrous consequences of this fatal error. If, he said, it be persisted in preventing silver from performing the historic *rôle* reserved to it, the commercial world will be subjected to a crisis more intense than any we can recollect. In addition to this, the diminution in the price of silver, which has fallen to 43d. the ounce, entails upon England and English trade, and all Government officials in India, losses which are attended with very grievous results. The Indian Treasury lost yearly on Council drawings £4,000,000; and at the present rate of exchange the loss would be more than £5,000,000. All Indian officials lose 30 per cent. in their exchanges for European money: and what is more serious still, the export trade with the East, and with all silver-standard countries, is subject to so much uncertainty that it has become wholly disorganised. No country suffers so much from all this as England.

"Again, the struggle for gold is simply death to free trade, for all Governments will raise their import duties, so as to keep as much gold at home as possible.

"Can this be the wish of English merchants and traders? There are two questions which put this debate on a very clear footing, and to which the opponents of bi-metallism will have some difficulty in replying: first, is one million sterling in gold sufficient to supply the growing monetary requirements of the entire world? And second, as in our Western world coinage has altogether ceased, and arts annually absorb £10,000,000 of the monetary stock, can things continue thus? It is clearly to the interest of Europe, and more especially of England, unhesitatingly to accept any proposal or hint coming from America to put in order the mechanism of international exchange; for, on the one hand, that country alone has nothing to lose, as she herself produces gold and silver, and at the same time absorbs a large portion of our gold, £25,000,000 in eight years; and, on the other, she has it in her power to crush the European money market in the most cruel manner. After the suspension of the Bland Act, which has now become inevitable, the price of silver will still further fall to 35d. per ounce, and perhaps even to 30d. per ounce. If America, making use of her profits made of late years on her monthly coinage of two millions of silver dollars, were to throw £20,000,000 of silver on the London market for sale, exacting gold payment, where should we all be? What value would silver have after that? And what would be the loss to India and to all traders with the East? And our banks, what would become of them?

" One essential point must not be lost sight of. It is not necessary for the establishment of international bi-metallism that any State should sacrifice its freedom of action as regards coinage, as was the case with the Latin Union. A common understanding between them would suffice; it is enough they should agree all to open their mints on the same day to the free coinage of the two metals, *with a fixed ratio of value between them.* None need undertake to continue this system for any length of time. If one State decide to abolish it, others can do so too, and it would be merely a return to the existing state of things; only an engagement should be entered upon that no State should take advantage of its neighbour's free coinage to secure gold in exchange for silver — a proceeding which would, indeed, bring no real advantage to itself.

" *Europe need never fear being overrun with American silver.* As one pound of silver would be worth the same amount of coin in the United States mints as in European, a holder of silver in America would have it coined and changed into gold there, if he so wished it. He would gain nothing by paying the cost of his silver crossing the Atlantic, as in Europe he would get no more for it than in America. As Newton very truly remarked, ' If the ratio between the two precious metals is everywhere the same, there is no advantage in sending away or in acquiring gold in preference to silver.' But even if Gresham's law retain any force of action, it would be applicable in America rather than anywhere else, because both metals are produced there.

"It seems that England has much to gain and nothing to lose in trying to come to an agreement with the other European States to give bi-metallism a fair trial."

The foregoing article, from the pen of M. de Laveleye, is typical of the attitude taken up by the silver party, and therefore it is useful to analyse it. The writer thinks that a chariot with one silver wheel and one gold one is preferable to having the wheels constructed of the same metal. Why, he does not inform us. "Coinage," we are told, "is the blood of the social body." It is quite evident that coinage is here confused with purchasing power. What is the use of coins, unless there is some agency to put them in motion ? What is the use of blood in the veins, unless there is introduced into the human body, by means of food, the heat and energy necessary to make it circulate ? We are told that "the quantity of gold sent by Australia to England is yearly diminishing," M. Laveleye apparently not having observed that of late years gold has been sent from Australia direct to the United States and other parts, instead of first coming to England, as was formerly the case. It is then stated that, "as for America, not only she no longer sends us any, but she yearly withdraws a portion from Europe." This is entirely incorrect, the greater part of the gold which has gone into the Bank of England during the past few months having come from the United States. We read that "the less gold there is the more it will appear superabundant, for the less there is the less it is required." Those who can reconcile the reasoning of the latter part of this quotation with the sustained complaint that the production of gold is unequal to requirements, must indeed possess a high order of reasoning power. What M. Laveleye says about trade with the East, and the loss sustained by Indian Civil Servants, is disposed of farther on, in Chapter VII. It is truly astonishing how erroneous have been the deductions hastily drawn in reference to the general monetary and trade operations between England and India. We are told that "the struggle for gold is death to free trade." M. de Laveleye is probably aware that the latest manifesto issued by a President of the United States was in favour of overthrowing the existing system of high tariffs and in favour of free trade, while evidence has been forthcoming in Germany and elsewhere to show that protection was a failure. We will conclude our criticism of this article by placing close to each other the following quotations: "If America, making use of her profits made of late years on her monthly coinage of two millions of silver dollars, were to throw £20,000,000 of silver on the London market for sale, exacting gold payment, where should we be?" A little farther on we read: "Europe need never fear being overrun with American silver."

The following sound remarks bearing on this question by Sir Lyon Playfair are worthy of a place where they can be more conveniently reperused than in the columns of even so widespread a journal as the *Times*, from which we have extracted them :—

"Sir Lyon Playfair, in responding to the toast, said he might perhaps make his remarks most useful by explaining why it was that there had been such a long and, with the exception of two years, 1880–81, nearly a continuous depression of manufactures since 1873. It was in such times of depression that protectionist policy tried to steady its flickering flame, and faint hearts among free-traders gave way to doubts. In his recent speech at Leeds he explained that the enormous improvements in locomotion by sea and by land had made the whole world the market for grain, and had profoundly altered our great agricultural industry. This cause had also operated partly to the advantage, partly to the disadvantage, of our own manufacturing industries, but it was not the main cause of their long-continued depression since 1873. There had been 12 periods of depression in this century, and formerly they were at pretty regular intervals of ten years; but this had altogether changed since 1873, and we ought to find out the reason. The first point to remark was that from 1873 to 1883 the depression was confined to machine-using countries, though after that date it gradually extended to hand-labour countries also. If we excluded Russia, there were 300 millions of inhabitants in machine-using countries and 1,000 millions in hand-labour countries. In the former the depression had been continuous and universal, whether they were at peace or war, whether they were protectionist or free trade in their policy. A universal result must have a universal cause, and that was what they had to seek. Since 1873 the progress of applied science had made astonishing developments. A development which needed centuries formerly for its consummation required, when he was young, decades, and now only involved years, and sometimes was at once complete. The telegraph had altered wholly our system of commerce, while railways and steamers had cheapened distribution enormously. There were now more than 300,000 miles of railways in the world, and this was equal to giving each inhabitant of the globe the powers which in old times he would have had by lending him the use of a horse for 12 working days in each year. In 1865, if a bale of goods had to be transported 1,000 miles by rail, 58 per cent. of its cost at the factory was swallowed up by transport; now only 20 per cent. was so consumed. Transport by sea, owing to the economy of fuel and labour, had been still more cheapened. The use of machinery had largely increased production, but it had at the same time displaced labour. A machine which did the work of ten men displaced nine labourers, though the wage of the machine worker was considerably raised. This displacement of labour was universal since 1873. In machine-made boots and shoes five-sixths of the old labour had been displaced. In agricultural implement making 600 men did now what 2,145 did in 1873; in milling corn, 75 per cent. of labour had been displaced, and in metal work about 33 per cent. Notwithstanding this displacement, production had largely increased, and so had the wages of the persons employed; but capital had had to be content with smaller profits. He would give one or two examples. In 1870 one man working at iron furnaces produced 170 tons of iron, and in 1885 he produced 260 tons. But in the introduction of new processes much capital and experience were lost. Thus steel, which was formerly made in puddling furnaces, was now produced in a wholly different way, and the capital of more than four and a-half millions invested in these furnaces was lost, while the labour of 39,000 men was displaced. It was the same case in many other manufactures. Thus coal-tar colours had substituted dyes imported from other countries, and whole crops had been swept away and the labour of their cultivators displaced. Irrespective of these actual changes produced by science, increased production by improved machinery, even in old manufactures, threw surplus stock on the markets of the world, and, as price was regulated by surplus, brought down profit to a *minimum*. Take the case of cotton manufactures as an illustration. In 1874 the speed of spindles was 4,000 revolutions per minute, but in 1885 it had become 10,000 revolutions. Consequently, more production could be obtained from the machines. But the product was altogether in excess of the growing population of the world, and was distinctly above the demand. A cheap supply of a commodity increased demand, but it did not immediately alter the habits of a people. A working man who was accustomed to wear one shirt per week would not, to accommodate the cotton trade, suddenly change his habits and wear one shirt every day, nor would his wife consent all at once to wash seven shirts weekly. Supply must not only suit demand, but must consult the habits of a population. This excess of supply over remunerative demand and price had left a very small margin of profit to the producer. At the same time, the more extended use of machinery had caused a profound alteration in domestic manufactures and handicrafts. The shoe-maker's trade was an example. Formerly the shoe-maker completed every part of a shoe, and was entire master of his craft. Now machinery had invaded this industry, and in the best manufactories there was much division of labour, about 64 different operations being carried on. Each operative in the manufactory, instead of being a complete shoemaker, was only 1-64th part of one. When new improvements lessened this division of work, the displaced workmen were thrown out, without having any complete vocation. He could not enter more fully into details; but he hoped they would now understand his point—that the universal cause which had produced the universal depression was that industry and commerce had not yet learnt how to adjust themselves to the advances of science, which had put at their disposal much more rapid and extensive means of production. What was the remedy? He could tell them first what was not the remedy. No nostrums of fair trade or protection would help us in the least. Those would simply put us in the bad position of protected countries, which contracted largely their intercourse with the markets of the world in order to shut out competition in their own domains. England for its prosperity largely depended on its export trade, and any restriction of that would be absolute ruin. Taxation on foreign commodities must be ultimately paid by the consumers in this country, and all taxation was a diminution from the strength of labour and from the fertility of the soil."

CHAPTER VII.

WE had intended summarising the first report of the Blue-Book on the Gold and Silver Commission, but the following from the *Economist* will save us the trouble.

On the Gold and Silver Commission there is no need to attempt to elaborate the case against the bi-metallists beyond what appeared in the *Economist*, as follows, on 6th August, 1887 :—

"THE GOLD AND SILVER COMMISSION.

" Last week we showed that no definite information, either as to the amount of the production of, or demand for, gold and silver, has been elicited by the inquiry of the Commission; nor have we gained from it any further insight into the movements of the prices of commodities. The result to which the investigations on this point have thus far led is, that the series of index numbers published in the *Economist* are about as reliable an indication of the movements in the prices of wholesale commodities as can be obtained. These index numbers are not to be taken as a perfectly accurate reflex of the variations in prices, both because they deal with only a limited number of commodities, and because it is impossible in compiling them to make exact allowance for the relative importance of the different articles. No one can be more fully sensible of their imperfection in these respects than we are, and we follow with interest the attempts that others have made to draw up a better record. What the Commission has found, however, is, that although there are points of difference between the *Economist* index numbers and those which other statisticians have drawn up, the broad results brought out are the same. And as regards what may be called the natural movement in prices, the *Economist* record is a much better guide than the records of prices which have been compiled in Germany and the United States, since prices in those countries have been materially influenced during late years by tariff changes. It may be well, therefore, to reproduce the table of index numbers for the past seventeen years.

" ' INDEX NUMBER ' REPRESENTING THE COMBINED PRICES OF TWENTY-TWO LEADING COMMODITIES.

Close of ..	1886	..	2,059	....	Close of ..	1877	..	2,529
,,	1885	..	2,023	....	,,	..	1876	..	2,723
,,	1884	..	2,098	....	,,	..	1875	..	2,711
,,	1883	..	2,221	....	,,	..	1874	..	2,778
,,	1882	..	2,342	....	,,	..	1873	..	2,891
,,	1881	..	2,435	....	,,	..	1872	..	2,947
,,	1880	..	2,376	....	,,	..	1871	..	2,835
,,	1879	..	2,538	....	,,	..	1870	..	2,591
,,	1878	..	2,202					

" Briefly stated, this shows a great rise of prices between 1870 and 1873, followed by an almost continuous fall till 1886, in which year there was a slight improvement. Unfortunately, there is no comprehensive record whatever of the movements in retail prices. We are thus left in doubt as to how far the purchasing power of gold in retail transactions has increased, and it is just in this retail business that the employment of gold is largest. The general conclusion, however, to which all available evidence on the part of the subject points is, that although retail prices have fallen, they have not fallen to the same extent as wholesale prices.

" Passing from the evidence as to the movements in prices to that portion of the inquiry which was directed towards eliciting information as to the alleged adverse effect upon trade of the fall in the gold price of silver, we come upon fresher ground, and to more definite conclusions. This is, of course, the most important part of the investigation, because, unless substantial injury can be shown to have resulted from the fall in silver, the schemes of the bi-metallists have no *raison d'être*, and on such a crucial point as this it may be well rather to let the witnesses speak for themselves, than to put any interpretation of our own upon what they did say. The first witness examined on this point was Mr. Henry Waterfield, the Financial Secretary at the Indian Office, whose evidence was brought to a point by Mr. Chamberlain, thus :—

" 1838. I understand that you consider that the fall in exchange is a great injury to the Government of India, and the people that it represents, but that it does not materially affect traders with India ?— That is my view.

" 1839. Or producers in India ?—I think that perhaps to some extent it is of advantage to the producers as distinguished from the tax-payers. In so far as they are producers, I think they may get an advantage by the greater number of rupees which they receive for their produce, but as taxpayers, the tax-paying community, I should say, has to pay more taxes for its gold disbursements, and taking the country as a whole, I think there is no advantage.

" 1840. But the producers in India would not receive a greater number of rupees, would they? The purchasing value of the rupee in India having practically remained the same, they would receive, *cæteris paribus*, the same number of rupees for the same amount of produce that they have done?—Quite so.

" 1841. Therefore, if they benefit at all, it is only by natural advantages, or the railways, or similar things, which are independent of the fall or fluctuation in exchange?—Yes.

" 1842. But, as far as your opinion goes, neither the producers in India, nor the purchasers of Indian produce, nor the exporters of European goods to India, nor the Indian purchasers of European imports, are materially affected by the fall in exchange?—No, I think not, in the long run, at all.

" 1843. Then there is only one other class of people who are affected, and those are the *employés* in the civil administration; but they are beneficially affected, I think?—They are paid in rupees at the old rate; but in so far as they have to remit their savings to England, or, when they come on furlough, to draw their furlough pay in England, or when they take their pensions, if the pensions are payable in rupees, they are injured by the fall in exchange. If the pensions are payable in sterling, they receive the same sterling amount as before, and therefore I think are benefited.

" 1844. But the soldiers?—The soldiers are benefited—that is, the British soldiers.

" 1853. Therefore we come to this, that in your opinion the one ground for interference is the case of the Government of India?—It is the main ground, I think.

" It may perhaps be well to add that the reason why the English soldiers are said to have benefited is that their payment being calculated in gold, they get more rupees than before, and as the purchasing power of the rupee in India has not diminished, they have a greater command of commodities than formerly.

"This is what may be called official evidence, and what we have next to deal with is the evidence of persons actually engaged in trade with the East. Amongst these, the first to be examined was Mr. J. K. Bythell, a member of a Manchester firm, who thus described the mode in which business with India is conducted:—

"1905. I should like just to impress upon the Commission, first of all, that nearly all of the business now, since telegraphic communication was so perfect, is done simultaneously. There is very little produce shipped, I believe, from India for sale, on what you might call speculation, as merchants' speculation, and there are very few Manchester goods, I think, shipped to India in that way. Business is nearly all done either in execution of offers made, or through the exporter making offers in the currency of the country in which he sells. For instance, if we sell 1,000 bales of cotton to a man in England that will be at so much per pound delivered in England. Well, we do not sell that unless at the time we can contract for the cotton in India at a price fixed in rupees, sell our bills on England at an exchange which the bank for the time being will then fix for bills to be delivered when the produce is ready, and engage our freight, so that, if we can close those three operations in India, of course we have fixed our price in sterling, and if we get the price fixed per pound simultaneously from our buyer in Europe our transaction is closed, provided all parties to the contract fulfil it—provided we have no failure.

To this it was objected that, although the merchant might thus shift the possibility of loss off from his own shoulders, the risk would have to fall somewhere. But Mr. Bythell demurred.

"1908. I do not think so, because the banks who buy the one class of bill and sell the other put one transaction against the other, and keep themselves covered from day to day as nearly as possible, I believe. For instance, I believe if some bank manager here who had branches in the East had telegrams to-day that his managers at his branches had bought bills for forward delivery against produce to a very large extent, he would practically cover himself almost immediately in some shape or form here. He would either buy Council drafts from Government, or he would buy silver, or he would buy from day to day bills drawn from here against shipments to India.

" 1909. That is, the base of the whole is on a fixed exchange. Of course, I am only inferring what Eastern bankers' business is. I believe you would find that the exchange banks, with their head offices in London and their branches in the East, scarcely speculate at all. They put the imports against the exports ; and the silver and the Government Council drafts, bills drawn by the Secretary of State for India, virtually finance the balance.

In other words, the transaction, being completed by all parties at the exchange of the moment, is practically arranged at a fixed exchange, and no party to the transaction need run an uncovered risk.

" Mr. R. Barclay, who is a strong bi-metallist, agreed in the main with Mr. Bythell as to the possibility of eliminating from trade with India the speculative element so far as exchange is concerned, his statement being : —

" 2241. In the great bulk of your transactions you secure yourself against any speculative loss ?—As much as we can.

" 2242. And on the whole you succeed ?—Yes ; and without violent fluctuations, no doubt we would succeed.

This statement, however, he subsequently qualified by explaining that if from any cause a manufacturer is unable to complete his contract within the specified time, he becomes liable for any loss on exchange that the delay may cause, and that in this way he very frequently suffers loss.

" The possibility of guarding in all cases against loss on exchange was, however, denied by Mr. Paul F. Tidman, of the firm of McTaggant & Co., East India merchants, whose view of the subject may be gathered from the following : —

"2819. Some of the witnesses that we have examined have told us that the particular source of loss [alteration in exchange] is obviated by arrangement with the banks, and by telegraphic transfers, by which the merchant exporting to the East and from the East is saved from all loss? —Yes. I think, however, it must be evident to the Commission that there is a risk incurred if the article which a man must take in exchange for his goods falls in value between the time of the commencement of his operation and the close. That risk must be borne by somebody, and if I put it on to a bank I simply shift the risk, and the person who takes that risk makes me pay for it. But, as a matter of fact, you will find that, whereas it has been asserted that Eastern banks are always willing to take this risk, there are times out of number when they decline to do so, and when the purchase of goods is simply stopped because the merchant cannot make his arrangement for the exchange.

On the other hand, however, Mr. A. D. Provand, M.P., the only other person examined on the business side of the question, gave it as his opinion that the Indian merchant can always ' cover' himself, but that in trading with China and Japan it was impossible to do so, except at a relatively high cost.

"As to whether the fall in exchange has or has not stimulated the Indian export trade opinion differed. Mr. Bythell holds strongly (Q. 1933) that ' the fall in silver or the fall in exchange, put it in which way you like, has been a very great benefit to the Indian producer, and has largely helped to develop the export trade.' As to national loss or gain, Mr. Barclay is not quite clear.

"2422. Well, now, taking the broad view of the trade between the United Kingdom and India, has not the course of it been that we get from India a much larger valuation of commodities than we sent to India?—Yes.

" 2423. And we have been sending from year to year bullion, to make up part of the balance?—Yes.

" 2424. We buy commodities that we receive from India more cheaply than before?—Yes.

" 2425. That is gain?—To this country, yes.

" 2426. We sell the commodities that we send out more cheaply? —Yes.

" 2427. That may be a loss?—A loss.

" 2428. But if we get much more than we lose, and we make up part of the balance in silver, which is cheaper, is there not, on the whole, a balance of gain to the United Kingdom?—Yes, in a sense.

" 2429. Whatever Manchester or Lancashire may suffer, the United Kingdom gains?—In a sense, yes; but it is not merely a matter of balance; each may gain something as against its loss, and still both be greatly worse off than if these difficulties did not exist.

" 2430. Well, now turn our attention to India. In consequence of the same facts, India has been able to develop a very large and increasing manufacture and export of cotton goods to the East?—Yes.

" 2431. Is that a gain to India?—A gain to India.

" 2432. And what has India as a community lost?—As against that?

" 2433. Yes.—Nothing, as against that individually; Lancashire has lost.

" 2434. But you say the United Kingdom, as a whole, has gained?— By cheap produce.

" 2435. The result is that the United Kingdom, as a whole, has gained?—No, I do not admit that. I said that the price of things that we export has gone down; besides, cheap Indian produce would not compensate England for the loss of her cotton manufactures.

" 2436. India has gained through the fact that silver has become cheaper relatively to other commodities. Why should we be discontented, when we have a gain on both sides?—It is not easy proving things off hand, but you would find a difference.

This evidence may be left to speak for itself. Its general tenor is to show that trade with the East is quite capable

of accommodating itself to alterations in the exchangeable value of gold and silver; and that, while the fall in
silver has injured certain individuals and classes, it has
benefited others. Whether, if a balance could be struck
between the losses and the gain, the preponderance would
be on the side of the former or the latter is a question on
which opinions differ. For our part, we are inclined to
regard the net result of all such currency fluctuations
as adverse. But the question is, whether the loss or
inconvenience shown is so great as would warrant us in
entertaining revolutionary currency schemes, and to that
question the evidence laid before the Commission gives a
very emphatic negative. The case for bi-metallism has,
in fact, broken down completely, and in view of that
fact, it is hardly worth while to discuss again the schemes
of its supporters."

CHAPTER VIII.

CAUSES OF THE FALL IN THE PRICE OF TEA FROM 1863 TO 1877, TRACED STEP BY STEP FROM PUBLISHED CIRCULARS.

AMONG the positive evidence which we have adduced in support of our contention that the fall in prices under review has been due almost entirely to causes outside and independent of currency influences, we have investigated, step by step, the causes of the decline in the important article Tea. Messrs. W. J. and H. Thompson were kind enough to let us have their file of circulars from 1863 to 1877, and we have shown, by extracts from these circulars, what have been the specific causes of the fall in price in this article over that period. Those engaged in the Tea trade watched, as a matter of course, closely the effect of the causes described, and accepted with confidence the change in the market value, without feeling the slightest necessity of searching elsewhere, either in the channels in which gold and silver ebb and flow, or elsewhere within the currency domain, for any subtle or obscure causes of the fall. The reader who may be in doubt can here, in the article of tea, follow the fall almost $\frac{1}{2}$d. by $\frac{1}{2}$d. per lb., and feel the influence which is the cause of the depreciation without any suspicion arising in his mind that there is any necessity to look further for an explanation. In the case of tea, the reduction in the duty had a good deal to do with the fall in price. In May, 1863, the duty was reduced from 1s. 5d. to 1s., having ruled at 1s. 5d. since 5th May, 1857, and in May, 1865, it was again reduced from 1s. to 6d. The retail trade at once lowered their prices 6d. per lb. As with tea, so it is in most other articles, as we have shown in the investigation by Mr. David A. Wells.

TEA.

Messrs. W. J. & H. Thompson's Annual Report of 8th January, 1863, states :—

Imports in 1862—106,500,000 lbs., against 92,750,000 lbs. in 1861.

Deliveries for exportation—27,500,000 lbs., against 13,950,000 lbs. in 1861.

Imports—13¼ million lbs. more than last year, but only equal to our requirements.

Exports—A surplus of no less than 13½ million lbs., caused by large demands for Canada, United States, with large additional shipments to Russia.

A comparison of prices ruling at the close of the year 1862 shows a fall ranging from 1d. per lb. up to 8d. per lb. over ten different sorts, and a rise ranging from 1d. per lb. up to 5d. per lb. over six different sorts.

Next circular of same date, referring to past month, states that new imports have stiffened in price, whilst most of the old were difficult of sale, even at easier rates. Comparing prices for the month, black tea showed no alteration, but in some descriptions of greens there was a fall of 2d. per lb.

Circular, 7th February, 1863.

Prices of several descriptions materially enhanced. Speculative buying was stimulated by growing opinion that there would be some reduction in amount of Customs duty. Stock showed sudden large increase.

Circular, 6th March, 1863.

Speculation referred to above soon abated, and moderate business followed at reduced prices. Stock again largely increased. Chancellor of Exchequer stated he had no reliable data at present for his calculation of surplus revenue.

Circular, 8th April, 1863.

Very limited business, in view of Budget being brought forward. No material alteration in prices.

Circular, 8th May, 1863.

Long-promised reduction of tea duty announced; all payments from 25th ultimo have been made at rate of 1s. per lb., in place of 1s. 5d. per lb. Prices settled down at 1d. to 3d. per lb. rise on settlement of this question.

Circular, 9th June, 1863.

Prices decidedly lower for the month. Great disinclination to purchase on the part of the dealers. Market flat and depressed.

Circular, 9th July, 1863.

Market continued in a state of considerable depression, with a lower range of prices for almost all kinds.

Circular, 8th August, 1863.

Arrivals heavy. Attention directed to public sale of 12,472 packages, put up " without reserve." Holders of new and old imports again accepted lower prices for medium sorts, fine remaining about the same. Prices all lower about 1d. per lb.

Circular, 9th September, 1863.

Market had been dull and inactive, it being found necessary to accept lower prices to effect sales. Stock increase of 21 million lbs., compared with same month 1862.

Circular, 9th October, 1863.

Large new arrivals freely offered, but comparatively few sales made. Prices show little alteration, except greens, which advanced 2d. per lb. Stock increase, 18 million lbs.

Circular, 9th November, 1863.

Fair business done in several instances at higher prices. Arrivals very numerous. Stock increase over 1862, 12 million lbs.

Circular, 9th December, 1863.

Small business done. Public sales unusually large. Double rise in Bank rate and stringency in money, causing very serious fall. Stock, 23 million lbs. increase.

Annual Report for 8*th January*, 1864, *says :*

Notwithstanding the long-expected boon of the reduction of duty to 1s. per lb., dealers have reason to recollect 1863, save during the earlier months, as a time chiefly of *heavy and continuous loss.* Large speculative purchases, made in a rising market prior to reduction in duty, had mainly to be realised when all were sellers, while the numerous arrivals and the accounts of further extended purchases in China, and over-sanguine views as to newly-opened trade with Russia, led, month after month, to increased heaviness.

	1863.		1862.
Imports..	136,500,000 lbs.,	against	106,500,000 lbs.
Home consumption	85,500,000 ,,	,,	78,750,000 ,,
Exports..	27,250,000 ,,	,,	27,500,000 ,,
Stock	89,000,000 ,,	,,	65,250,000 ,,

On comparing prices, 1863 showed a fall of from 1d. to 5d. per lb. over eleven different sorts, and a rise of 2d. to 4d. per lb. over three different sorts.

Circular, 9*th January*, 1864.

Arrivals numerous. Business very moderate at unaltered prices. Stock, 24 million lbs. increase against same month last year.

Circular, 9*th February*, 1864.

Market quiet; public sales not large. Prices of medium blacks rather lower, but several descriptions of greens advanced 1d. to 2d. per lb. Stock, 22 million lbs. increase.

Circular, 9*th March*, 1864.

Arrivals unusually numerous. Business fair, and some common descriptions realised rather better prices, but medium and good kinds rather lower.

Circular, 9*th April*, 1864.

Steady course of market, with prices unchanged. Stock increase against same time 1863, 22 million lbs.

Circular, 9*th May*, 1864.

Lower and medium grades of Congou declined $\frac{1}{2}$d. to 1d. per lb. Very moderate extent of business. Chief feature, large public sales. All orders from United States cancelled, owing to expected large addition to import duty there. Bank rate raised to 8 per cent. on the 2nd, and to 9 per cent. on the 5th inst.

Circular, 9th June, 1864.

Business was checked by the higher prices required by importers, and demand, which had been increasing, greatly subsided. Prices showed ½d. per lb. advance on common, and ½d. to 1d. per lb. on medium Congou. Stock increase of 19 million lbs.

Circular, 9th July, 1864.

Market languid. Business difficult. Public sales small, but, nevertheless, they went off flatly, showing a slight decline in commonest Congous.

Circular, 9th August, 1864.

Prices further receded, and the private market was dull and inactive ; all green descriptions were also lower.

Circular, 9th September, 1864.

Business very limited. Lower prices ruled at public auctions. Bank rate raised to 9 per cent. on 8th inst. Stock, 2 million lbs. increase.

Circular, 8th October, 1864.

Private market for old imports dull and inactive, but no change in prices.

Circular, 9th November, 1864.

Cessation of arrivals created somewhat firmer market, aided by some speculative purchases. Prices of most kinds of medium Congous again lower. Stock, 18 million lbs. increase against 1863.

Circular, 9th December, 1864.

Business small and difficult. Inferior kinds put freely on the market, and prices receded fully 1d. per lb. Prices of medium Congous declined 1d. per lb.

Annual Report, 7th January, 1865.

Severe loss to import trade, owing to unduly high cost and depression at home. Excepting a short period in the Spring, prices in all but the finer qualities declined, the fall accelerated by money pressure.

	1864.	1863.
Imports	123,000,000 lbs., against	136,500,000 lbs.
Home consumption	88,500,000 ,, ,,	85,500,000 ,,
Exports	28,500,000 ,, ,,	27,250,000 ,,

Circular, 9th January, 1865.

Little change on month.   Prices unaltered.

Circular, 9th February, 1865.

Arrivals numerous.   Disinclination of trade to buy.   Common Congous full 1d. per lb. lower, also several kinds of green.   Stock, 6 million lbs. increase compared with February, 1864.

Circular, 9th March, 1865.

Market remained in same stagnant state, sales showing further reductions in several qualities.   Stock, 17 million lbs. increase.

Circular, 8th April, 1865.

Less pressure to sell, imparting rather firmer tone to market. Prices, however, remained generally unchanged.   Stock, 11 million lbs. increase.

Circular, 9th May, 1865.

The publication of the Budget on the 28th ult., reducing the duty from 1s. to 6d. per lb., caused sudden excitement.   In many cases importers refused to sell even at 2d. per lb. over previous quotations.   Chief supply drawn from the stocks of the larger dealers.   For two days a fair extent of business was done at an advance of 1d. to $1\frac{1}{2}$d. per lb. on fair to medium, and fully 2d. per lb. on fine qualities of Congou, but at the public sales prices declined, Chancellor having agreed to postpone alteration of duty until June 1st.   Market became languid. Stock, 4 million lbs. increase.

Circular, 9th June, 1865.

Prices unaltered, holidays and large clearances causing almost a cessation of business.

Circular, 8th July, 1865.

Market dull and inactive.   Large public sales on importers' account marked " without reserve."   Tendency of prices downwards.   Common and fair Congou $\frac{1}{2}$d. to 1d. per lb. lower, and common greens about 1d. lower.   Stock, 500,000 lbs. as compared with July, 1864.

Circular, 9th August, 1865.

Prices for Congous unaltered.   Market unchanged.

Circular, 9th September, 1865.

Private contract market firmer, and public sales passed off more satisfactorily.   Fine shipping green teas dearer, but common kinds slightly lower.

Circular, 9th October, 1865.

Prices unaltered. Business fair.

Circular, 9th November, 1865.

Market firmer and active, at an *advance* in prices for most kinds, both dealers and speculators operating freely.   Congous 1d. per lb. higher ; Monings and Oolongs 1d. to 2d. dearer.

Circular, 9th December, 1865.

Fine " new " import Congous 1d. lower, and second class and medium even lower.   " Old " imports unaltered.   Stock, 16 million lbs. decrease.

Annual Report of 8th January, 1866, states :

The year 1865 will long be remembered for the accumulated losses on the import of tea, owing to the continuous excess of supply, and the extreme prices paid, leading to the ruin of many old-established firms. Reaction in latter part of year, stimulated by unexpected reduction of duty to 6d. per lb., the general prosperity of the working classes causing a rapid increase in the consumption, while export demand was largely augmented by the sudden peace in America.   On the reduction of the duty the retail trade at once lowered their prices 6d. per lb., causing a demand for quality and enquiry for new teas to exclusion of old.

	1865.		1864.
Imports..	116,000,000 lbs.,	against	123,000,000 lbs.
Home consumption	98,000,000 ,,	,,	88,000,000 ,,
Exports..	33,000,000 ,,	,,	28,500,000 ,,
Stock	80,000,000 ,,	,,	95,000,000 ,,

On the year prices rose all round, ranging from 1½d. per lb. to 6d. per lb.

Circular, 9th January, 1866.

Fair business.   Prices for medium and second-class Congous 1d. to 2d. per lb. lower.   Stock, 15 million lbs. increase against January, 1865. Bank rate raised to 8 per cent. on 4th.

Circular, 9th February, 1866.

Fair business ; but the lower qualities most difficult to realise at a further decline in some cases.   Better sorts of black leaf advanced fully 1d. per lb.   Stock, 12 million lbs. decrease.

Circular, 9th March, 1866.

Market extremely quiet, and prices are maintained.

Circular, 9th April, 1866.

Easter holidays. Markets quiet. Congous unaltered, but finest gunpowder 1d. to 2d. per lb. lower. Stock, 12 million lbs. decrease.

Circular, 9th May, 1866.

Last fortnight one of continued depression and inactivity, importers, however, not pressing sales. Intense panic prevailing in all financial matters. Prices unaltered.

Circular, 9th June, 1866.

Bank rate continued at 10 per cent. Tea market tolerably firm. Prices nominally unaltered, but sales occasionally made at lower rates. Stock, 13 million lbs. decrease.

Circular, 9th July, 1866.

No improvement in the market. Fair quality Congou ½d. to 1d. per lb. lower. Oolongs and common greens ½d. per lb. lower, but Hysons 2d. per lb. lower.

Circular, 9th August, 1866.

No improvement. Business restricted. Considerable sales without reserve. Bank rate still 10 per cent. Prices generally unaltered. Stock, 8 million lbs. decrease.

Circular, 8th September, 1866.

Little doing beyond attention given to large public sale " without reserve." Bank rate down to 5 per cent. Owing to pressure of sales prices generally reduced.

Circular, 9th October, 1866.

Slight improvement during last fortnight. More business doing at better prices. Common black leaf Congous rather dearer. Scented teas 1d. per lb. lower.

Circular, 9th November, 1866.

Extremely heavy market, with Congous of old import ½d. to 1d. per lb. lower; Kaisows of new import 1d. to 2d. per lb. lower. Monings, 3d. per lb. lower. Tayshans and scented teas 1d. per lb. lower. Stock, 4 million lbs. decrease.

Circular, 9th December, 1866.

Slightly better feeling, and prices rallied 1d. to 2d. per lb., followed, however, by the greatest dulness, fair and medium at the end being 1d. to 2d. per lb. lower.

The Annual Circular of 8th January, 1867, says:

The course of the year has been marked by no ordinary events: war, pestilence, panics, both financial and commercial, the failure of banks and of some firms previously enjoying the highest reputation, creating for the time an amount of distress and distrust almost unparalleled. To importers and holders of tea generally it has been one of heavy loss. The fall in some classes during the year was no less than 6d. to 8d. per lb., much of which was occasioned by the extreme contract prices paid in China, especially for contract teas, notwithstanding a general inferiority in quality, regardless of the large surplus export which was hurried forward in the early part of the season, in the face of the certainty of its causing a glut at home.

It is important here to note what Messrs. Thompson call particular attention to in this circular, because it is in this, as in other trades, the beginning of a *new departure*, arising out of the extension of the telegraphic system, and the better means of communication and transport, which at this period commenced to revolutionise the commerce of the world, and to eliminate the middleman, whose large intermediary profits had for so long kept up prices at an unduly high level, thereby laying an unfair and unjust burden upon all consumers. With the development of this new departure an element was eliminated, the absence of which must of necessity be in itself the cause of a fall in all prices, for it is well known that all intermediary profits over and above that of the producer adds to the price paid by the consumer. Not only, therefore, has the elimination of the merchant and other form of middleman conduced to the general fall in prices which has been going on of late years, but it has occurred concurrently with largely increased production of all the great staples of commerce, and a very material reduction in the cost of transit from the producer to the consumer or retail trader. Concurrently, again, with the development of this new departure, the general welfare of the inhabitants of the world has so vastly improved, that the cash payment system has been able to establish itself and break down the grinding tyranny of credit. The necessaries of life people must have, and while the supply of them was kept under the control of " rings " the consumer was mulcted of 20, 30 and sometimes 50 per cent. more than the article he bought was worth. The barriers enabling the merchant and producer to do this have been thrown down, and what is the result to-day? Producers and merchants, and the great army that distributes the article to the public that consumes it, are continually crying out for Royal Commissions of Inquiry and for the re-establishment of bi-metallism. For a very long time these gentlemen have enjoyed themselves in the warm corners of the world, but their time has come to turn out.

The imports during the past year into the United Kingdom have been .. .. 139,000,000 lbs., against 116,000,000 lbs. in 1865
The deliveries for home consump- 102,000,000 ,, ,, 98,000,000 ,, ,, tion .. ..
Exportation .. 31,000,000 ,, ,, 33,100,000 ,, ,,
The imports were thus 23 millions more than last year, and six millions more than our deliveries.

Circular, 9th January, 1867.

Prices in some cases 1d. per lb. higher. Very fair business. Stock, increase of 9 million lbs. compared with December, 1865.

Circular, 9th February, 1867.

Business moderate. Prices unaltered. Stock, 4½ million lbs. increase.

Circular, 9th March, 1867.

Market had been extremely dull. Prices fully ½d. per lb. lower. Stock, 1½ million lbs. increase.

Circular, 9th April, 1867.

Increased heaviness. Quantity offering more than requirements. Prices ½d. to 1d. per lb. lower. Stock, 12 million lbs. lower than corresponding period 1866.

Circular, 9th May, 1867.

Improving tendency in prices. Stock, 14 million lbs. lower.

Circular, 8th June, 1867.

No change. Stock, 4 million lbs. lower.

Circular, 9th July, 1867.

Devoid of animation. Prices slightly lower. Stock, 1½ million lbs. lower.

Circular, 9th August, 1867.

Dull and depressed. Prices for some descriptions again a little lower. Stock, 11¼ million lbs. lower.

Circular, 9th September, 1867.

Business limited. Congous unaltered in price, but scented Capers and coloured Japans, 1d. to 2d. per lb. lower.

Circular, 9th October, 1867.

Numerous arrivals. More animation. Prices for fine Congous fully maintained. Superior and medium, 1d. per lb. lower. Stock, 12½ million lbs. lower.

Circular, 9th November, 1867.

Market generally quiet, some descriptions 1d. per lb. lower. Stock, 7 million lbs. lower.

Circular, 9th December, 1867.

Continued dulness in the market. Some descriptions again lower. Stock, 17 million lbs. lower than for corresponding period of 1866.

The Annual Circular of 8th January, 1868, *says :*

Increasing deliveries. Supplies in the aggregate considerably below them. Largely reduced stock should under ordinary circumstances have had a favourable influence in prices. But increased dulness prevailed, only enlivened by arrival of new crop. Even then, demand only spasmodic, a reaction almost invariably following each advance, so that prices on about the same level at close of 1866.

Imports	124,750,000 lbs., against	139,000,000 lbs. in 1866.
Deliveries for home consumption ..	111,000,000 ,, ,,	102,000,000 ,, ,,
Exports	32,000,000 ,, ,,	31,000,000 ,, ,,

Circular, 9th January, 1868.

Improved demand, but arrivals considerable. Some descriptions 1d. per lb. lower. Stock for last month of 1867, 18 million lbs. lower than in January, 1866.

Circular, 8th February, 1868.

Decided signs of improvement. Prices for siftings and broken leaf ¼d. per lb., and fair grades Congou ½d. to 1d. per lb. dearer.

Circular, 5th March, 1868.

Market quiet and transactions moderate. Prices ½d. per lb. lower in some cases. Canton and Scented Orange Pekoes ½d. per lb. dearer. Stock, 13¼ million lbs. lower.

Circular, 8th April, 1868.

Considerable activity. Dealers as well as speculators operating freely. Prices for all common to medium grades of Congou advanced ½d. to 1d. per lb. Stock, 10½ million lbs. lower.

Circular, 7th May, 1868.

Market very quiet. Fear of increased duty since introduction of Budget, coupled with latest China advices, causing importers to hold, owing to anticipated heavy clearances. Siftings and broken leaf ½d. to 1d. per lb. higher, and common Congous slightly dearer. Stock, 9½ million lbs. lower.

Circular, 4th June, 1868.

Market extremely quiet. Prices slightly dearer. Stock, 12 million lbs. lower.

Circular, 2nd July, 1868.

Unusually quiet. Prices, where any changes, slightly lower. Stock, 4½ million lbs. lower.

Circular, 13th August, 1868.

No change. Prices again ruled lower for all kinds. Stock, 12½ million lbs. lower.

Circular, 10th September, 1868.

Notwithstanding arrival of new season's teas, business very small. Where any changes, prices again lower. Stock, 9½ million lbs. lower.

Circular, 8th October, 1868.

Greatest inactivity prevailed. Nothing but good and fine sorts saleable. Prices of fair to medium Foochow teas, of new import, 1d. to 2d. per lb. lower. Scented and green teas also lower. Stock, 7 million lbs. lower.

Circular, 5th November, 1868.

A fair business transacted. Prices without change. Stock, 11 million lbs. lower than at corresponding period of 1867.

Circular, 3rd December, 1868.

Dull and unsatisfactory market. Prices, where any change, ½d. to 1d. per lb. lower. Stock, 6½ million lbs. increase.

Annual Report, 13*th January*, 1869.

Severe fluctuations experienced during the past year. Opened under the influence of extended deliveries and decreasing stocks. Stock stood at 64 million lbs.—lower than it had been since 1862. A worse feature even than the market being flooded with arrivals was the result of inferior quality.

The following is deserving of special attention:—" If it is to be admitted that the altered relations of trade in China will in future necessitate an *overwhelming* supply during the early months, the position at home must also be realised, viz., *that with the increasing rapidity of communication and freeness of transit, the necessity of any but a moderate stock is a thing of the past; that large exports from China will inevitably* DEPRESS PRICES *at home*, for a time at least; and that, therefore, if the trade hereafter is to be a remunerative one, there must be a radical change in the mode of buying, in the rates paid, and in the quality purchased. The present system holds out a premium to the Chinese to make bad tea, and has been the fertile source of ruinous loss."

Imports	..	..	153,000,000 lbs.,	against 125,000,000 lbs. in 1867
Deliveries ..		..	106,000,000 ,,	,, 111,000,000 ,, ,,
Exports	..	..	36,000,000 ,,	,, 32,000,000 ,, ,,
Stock on 31st Dec.			88,000,000 ,,	,, 77,000,000 ,, ,,

Circular, 15*th January*, 1869.

Moderate demand. Much larger quantity offering than can be taken by the dealers. Prices ½d. to 1d. per lb. lower. (On 31st ult.) Stock, 88 million lbs., against 77 million lbs. in 1867.

Circular, 11*th February*, 1869.

Steadier market. Demand had continued good. Common Congou ¼d. to ½d. per lb. dearer. Other kinds unaltered. Stock, 100 million lbs., against 86 million lbs. in 1868.

Circular, 17*th March*, 1869.

No material change. Prices ¼d. to ½d. per lb. lower. Stock, 104 million lbs., against 87 million lbs. in 1868.

Circular, 8*th April*, 1869.

A fair demand experienced since the Easter holidays. Scented kinds 1d. per lb. lower. Common Congou rather firmer. Most good kinds and fine very irregular. Stock, 102 million lbs., against ·88 million lbs. in 1868.

Circular, 6th May, 1869.

Market had shown further signs of depression, and prices were again lower for all descriptions, the pressure to realise being greater than the trade could withstand. Auctions very large. Stock, 99 million lbs., against 81 million lbs. in 1868.

Circular, 3rd June, 1869.

Improved tone, with much better demand. Prices scarcely affected, but fair and common Congous about ½d. per lb. dearer. Stock, 92 million lbs., against 84 million lbs. in 1868.

Circular, 7th July, 1869.

Little change either in tone of market or in prices. Stock, 86 million lbs., against 77 million lbs. in 1868.

Circular, 4th August, 1869.

Market firm, but few transactions. Prices firm, but unchanged. Stock, 75 million lbs., against 70 million lbs. in 1868.

Circular, 9th September, 1869.

Demand had been strong for flavoury qualities. All grades freely taken. New Season's Moning Congou about 1d. per lb. lower for medium grades. Others unaltered. Stock, 68 million lbs., against 64 million lbs. in 1868.

Circular, 7th October, 1869.

Since our last, with one interval, there have been public sales each day, increasing the panic, and showing differences now extending from 5d. to 6d. per lb. from the opening prices, and in the individual cases of 2d. to 3d. per lb. within a week. The irregularities in price are greater than ever known, much to the interest of buyers. The Private Contract market is entirely disorganised, and nothing but teas with point, for which high prices are paid and large profits secured, are practically saleable.

Prices 1d. to 2d. per lb. lower for ordinary grades. Oolongs 3d. to 4d. per lb. lower than opening rates. Stock, 68 million lbs., against 65 million lbs. in 1868,

Circular, 4th November, 1869.

Market had been particularly dull and without animation. For the majority of parcels lower prices continue to be accepted. The public auctions closed with heaviness. Stock, 72 million lbs., against 67 million lbs. in 1868.

Circular, 2nd December, 1869.

Market had continued dull and heavy, and prices continued to droop for all medium prices. Stock, 78 million lbs., against 81 million lbs. in 1868.

Annual Report, 12th January, 1870.

On the bulk of the operations of the past year the result had been loss and disappointment. The chief experiences were pressure to realise, led by several public sales " without reserve," advertised as each vessel was reported. This action induced almost panic. Most importers have been eager to sell, frightened by the *fearful reduction in the value of old stock.* It was pointed out that " teas will be brought forward both earlier and in larger quantities than before, that importers will sell on arrival, that dealers, warned by the experience of each year, will confine their buyings to their immediate wants." Hopes of revival in trade increase as the disasters of 1866 are further removed by lapse of time.

Imports .. .. .. 145,000,000 lbs.,against 153,000,000 lbs. in 1868
Deliveries .. .. 111,000,000 ,, ,, 106,000,000 ,, ,,
Exportation .. .. 34,000,000 ,, ,, 35,000,000 ,, ,,
Stock, 31st inst. .. 87,000,000 ,, ,, 88,000,000 ,, ,,

Circular, 13th January, 1870.

Decided improvement in tone of market since commencement of year. Large quantity of tea brought forward, but price of good Congou slightly firmer. Good medium to fine Monings 1d. per lb. dearer. Stock, 87 million lbs., against 88 million lbs. in 1868.

Circular, 10th February, 1870.

Arrivals during last fortnight very numerous. Prices did not give way, but sales difficult. Stock, 89 million lbs., against 100 million lbs. in 1869.

Circular, 13th April, 1870.

Publication of Budget on 11th inst. caused increased flatness in the market. Prices unaltered. Stock, 107 million lbs., against 102 million lbs. in 1869,

Circular, 12th May, 1870.

Market during past few days has continued very flat, owing to the large sales by public auction and to further sales advertised ; dealers only buying when forced. Prices unaltered. Stock, 107 million lbs., against 99 million lbs. in 1869.

Circular, 9th June, 1870.

Holidays and discussions on the importers' alterations in the conditions of sale chiefly occupied the attention of the trade. Prices nominally unaltered. Stock, 101 million lbs., against 92 million lbs. in 1869.

Circular, 7th July, 1870.

Little business beyond public auctions. Prices without change. Stock, 92 million lbs., against 86 million lbs. in 1869.

Circular, 4th August, 1870.

Moderate business, without change in prices since alterations in conditions of sale. Stock, 79 million lbs., against 75 million lbs. in 1869.

Circular, 1st September, 1870.

Good business in new arrivals, but prices of inferior common black, of old import, ½d. to 1d. per lb. lower. The finer grades of new season's teas firmer. Stock, 79 million lbs., against 75 million lbs. in 1869.

Circular, 6th October, 1870.

Market continued firm. Prices unchanged. Stock, 73 million lbs., against 68 million lbs. in 1869.

Circular, 3rd November, 1870.

Good amount of business had been transacted. Prices for medium black and red leaf firm ; fine black leaf and scented teas 1d. per lb. lower. Stock, 72 million lbs., against 68 million lbs. in 1869.

Circular, 1st December, 1870.

Market had been very quiet. Few sales effected showed great irregularity, partly owing to decrease of orders from the country, and partly to the quantity forced forward. Prices for common red and black leaf ½d. per lb. lower, and medium black leaf 1d. per lb. lower. Stock, 76 million lbs., against 78 million lbs. in 1869.

Annual Circular, 11*th January*, 1871.

Results of the course of the trade for the past year, on the whole, satisfactory. In the earlier months the market was influenced by the expectation of some alteration in the duty, and prices suffered when it was ascertained there would not be any reduction. Heavy arrivals taking place at the time also contributed to the general dulness. *Deliveries of Indian teas had increased in the year about* 3 *millions of lbs.* The imports show an equal advance, owing to the heavy shipments *viâ* the Suez Canal. Indian tea in increasing favour.

Imports .. .. 140,000,000 lbs., against 145,000,000 lbs. in 1869
Deliveries .. .. 117,000,000 „ „ 111,000,000 „ „
Exportation .. 30,000,000 „ „ 34,000,000 „ „

Circular, 12*th January*, 1871.

Attention of dealers directed to stocktaking. Prices showed a slight decline. (On 30th ultimo, 1870) Stock, 79 million lbs., against 87 million lbs. in 1869.

Circular, 9*th February*, 1871.

Trade quiet. More offering than could be taken by the trade. Prices for common to full grades of Congou rather weaker; good and fine firmer. Stock, 90 million lbs., against 89 million lbs. in 1870.

Circular, 9*th March*, 1871.

Rather more activity in the market. Prices irregular, but no material change. Stock, 98 million lbs., against 100 million lbs. in 1870.

Circular, 5*th April*, 1871.

No activity, with prices occasionally in favour of buyers. Green teas also lower. Stock, 96 million lbs., against 107 million lbs. in 1870.

Circular, 4*th May*, 1871.

Market had been extremely dull. Dealers engaged in clearing largely, fearing an increased duty. Prices for commonest grades of Congou, green teas and scented Capers ½d. to 1d. per lb. lower. Stock, 97 million lbs., against 107 million lbs. in 1870.

Circular, 1*st June*, 1871.

Market continued firm. Extent of business limited. Deliveries on satisfactory scale. Prices for common to fair grades of Congou dearer. Stock, 89 million lbs., against 101 million lbs. in 1870.

Circular, 13*th July*, 1871.

Market had been particularly quiet. Only feature public sale, at which several parcels of good to fine Monings were sold at reduced rates. Prices for good to fine black leaf and Taysham Congous of medium quality 1d. to 2d. per lb. lower. Stock, 82 million lbs., against 92 million lbs. in 1870.

Circular, 10*th August*, 1871.

Arrival of new season's teas being disappointing in quality, several chops were sold at public auction fully 3d. per lb. below the first few sales made. Stock, 71 million lbs., against 79 million lbs. in 1870.

Circular, 7*th September*, 1871.

Steadier market and more general business. Prices of common Congou ½d. per lb. lower ; fair to medium new brown leaf 1d. per lb., Oolongs 2d. per lb. lower ; scented teas also lower. Stock, 79 million lbs., against 74 million lbs. in 1870.

Circular, 5*th October*, 1871.

Market had been firm, with more business doing last week, excepting inferior to common black leaf Congous, which were lower. Stock, 78 million lbs., against 73 million lbs. in 1870.

Circular, 2*nd November*, 1871.

Demand good, but business had been limited. Prices generally unaltered. Stock, 73 million lbs., against 72 million lbs. in 1870.

Circular, 14*th December*, 1871.

Tone had been quiet, with small business. Prices unaltered. Stock, 82 million lbs., against 76 million lbs. in 1870.

Annual Report, 3*rd January*, 1872.

During past year deliveries had shown an unprecedented increase ; on the one hand showing an elasticity in the consumption, consequent on the low rate of duty, and on the other affording reassuring evidence to those who feared that our export trade would decline owing to the direct communication by steamers now established between Russia and China. The result at one time threatened to be serious to importers, for not only was the system of hurrying forward the new crop by the Suez Canal carried to a dangerous extent, but much higher prices were paid to China than the quality warranted, and as a natural consequence, under the pressure to realise, some sharp losses were at first experienced. Home consumption had been stimulated by the *low retail price.* Market was beginning to be affected by increasing imports from India, the general improvement in quality enabling the dealers to mix most advantageously.

Imports	167,000,000 lbs., against 140,000,000 lbs. in 1870		
Deliveries for home consumption ..	123,000,000 ,,	,, 117,000,000 ,,	,,
Exports	40,000,000 ,,	,, 30,000,000 ,,	,,
Stock (31st Dec.)..	83,000,000 ,,	,, 79,000,000 ,,	,,

Circular, 11th January, 1872.

Had been numerous arrivals. Large quantity offering. Demand had been fair. Prices irregular, and frequently ½d. per lb. lower. Scented orange Pekoe ½d. per lb. dearer. Stock (31st ult.), 83 million lbs., against 79 million lbs. in 1870.

Circular, 1st February, 1872.

Market steady, but business moderate. Prices for Congous unaltered. Green teas 1d. per lb. dearer. Stock (31st ult.), 83 million lbs., against 79 million lbs. in 1870.

Circular, 7th March, 1872.

Large quantity had been brought forward. Tone of market consequently dull. Prices lower all round ½d. to 1d. per lb. Stock, 93 million lbs., against 98 million lbs. in 1871.

Circular, 4th April, 1872.

Easter holidays. Business quiet. Prices unaltered. Stock, 103 million lbs., against 96 million lbs. in 1871.

Circular, 2nd May, 1872.

No improvement in market. Prices irregular and occasionally lower. Stock, 100 million lbs., against 97 million lbs. in 1871.

Circular, 6th June, 1872.

Market continued dull and heavy. Large quantities brought forward at auction. Prices generally ½d. per lb. lower. Stock, 90 million lbs., against 89 million lbs. in 1871.

Circular, 4th July, 1872.

Market continued extremely dull. Prices unaltered. Stock, 78 million lbs., against 82 million lbs. in 1871.

Circular, 1st August, 1872.

Quantity offering very large. Prices unaltered. Stock, 78 million lbs., against 82 million lbs. in 1871.

Circular, 5th September, 1872.

Market had continued quiet. Prices generally unaltered. Stock, 87 million lbs., against 79 million lbs. in 1871.

Circular, 3rd October, 1872.

Market had relapsed into a quiet state, after being better. Some kinds a little dearer, but prices mostly unchanged. Stock, 82 million lbs., against 78 million lbs. in 1871.

Circular, 7th November, 1872.

Business had been limited. Prices, where any change, lower. Stock, 83 million lbs., against 73 million lbs. in 1871.

Circular, 5th December, 1872.

Market had been quiet, and sales difficult to effect at the reduced prices. Prices without change, except for district green teas, which were 1d. to 2d. per lb. lower. Stock, 88 million lbs., against 82 million lbs. in 1871.

Annual Report, 8th January, 1873.

Results of the past year had been anything but satisfactory, with the exception of the deliveries, owing to the high prices paid in China. It was remarked " that unless prices are on a level at which they can act without fear of loss, they will repeat their tactics of buying only from hand to mouth another year, and such must have a tendency to affect prices adversely, *more especially with the present system of hurried shipments, and the unexpected supplies from time to time by steamers.* Regarding *Indian teas*, it was remarked that they continued to increase in favour, *and must yearly exercise more and more influence upon the general prices of China tea."*

From the above remarks, it is quite evident that the price of tea was being steadily and continuously affected in buyers' favour, not only by larger production in China itself, and by the greater rapidity with which it could be brought to market, but also by the opening up of a new field of production, which was destined to be a competitor equal in the end, if not superior as a tea-growing country, to China itself. Messrs. Thompson, in their annual report, tell us that " Up to the present time, the increase in the quantity has been very gradual, but of late the extensions in the gardens have been on a large scale, which in four or five years must tell very materially. The pace at which this competition of Indian tea was growing is seen from the fact that of the 4½ million lbs. increase in home consumption, 2¾ million lbs. is due to Indian tea; in short, the rate of delivery has of late slightly exceeded that of the imports."

Imports   .. .. 182,000,000 lbs., against 167,000,000 lbs. in 1871
Deliveries .. .. 127,000,000 ,,   ,,   123,000,000 ,,   ,,
Exports   .. .. 39,000,000 ,,   ,,   40,000,000 ,,   ,,
Stock (31st ult.).. 98,000,000 ,,   ,,   83,000,000 ,,   ,,

Circular, 9th January, 1873.

Improved demand. All descriptions but Congous were dull, and prices in many cases lower. Stock (31st December), 98 million lbs., against 83 million lbs. in 1871.

Circular, 6th February, 1873.

Market quiet. Business small. Prices generally lower. Stock, 105 million lbs., against 92 million lbs. in 1872.

Circular, 6th March, 1873.

Heavy arrivals and absence of demand from the country had caused great depression in the market. At the auction prices very irregular, and in many instances lower. Stock, 101 million lbs., against 93 million lbs. in 1872.

Circular, 3rd April, 1873.

Business had been almost at a standstill, no improvement being looked for until after the Budget had been brought forward. No less than nine vessels had been reported. Congous unaltered, but medium grades of green ½d. to 1d. per lb. lower. Stock, 100 million lbs., against 103 million lbs. in 1872.

Circular, 1st May, 1873.

Fair business, without change in prices. Stock, 100 million lbs., against 103 million lbs. in 1872.

Circular, 5th June, 1873.

Business scarcely resumed since Whitsuntide holiday. Prices unchanged. Stock, 83 million lbs., against 90 million lbs. in 1872.

Circular, 3rd July, 1873.

Large falling off in exports, but a satisfactory increase in home consumption. Good to fair Congous ½d. per lb. dearer; other kinds unaltered. Stock, 72 million lbs., against 78 million lbs. in 1872.

Circular, 7th August, 1873.

Fair demand for Congous at unchanged prices, but scented teas generally 1d. per lb. lower. Stock, 68 million lbs., against 84 million lbs. in 1872.

Circular, 4th September, 1873.

Market dull and quiet. Congous irregular and occasionally lower. Stock, 73 million lbs., against 87 million lbs. in 1872.

Circular, 2nd October, 1873.

Market dull and quiet. Fair to medium grades of black leaf Congous show ½d. per lb. decline. Stock, 78 million lbs., against 82 million lbs. in 1872.

Circular, 6th November, 1873.

Same depression continued. Heavy arrivals and high price of money tended to reduce business to the smallest limits. At public auction prices again ruled lower. Stock, 84 million lbs., against 83 million lbs. in 1872.

Circular, 4th December, 1873.

Several arrivals during week, and a large quantity placed on the market. Prices unchanged.

Annual Report, 6th January, 1874.

Importers had experienced severe losses, owing to the extravagant prices paid last season for the second and third crops, though admitted to be of inferior quality; while with the great competition for the new crop this year, and the hurried manner in which, as of late, supplies were sent forward, there was little probability of making any profit. All the arrivals showed heavy losses. The passing of the Adulteration Act, by checking the import of inferior and spurious teas, had caused importers to suffer severely, and to an extent that could never have been contemplated by the Legislature. The exports had fallen off, owing to the increase in the direct shipments to Russia, and a feature in the development of the trade was the further increase of 4 millions in the home consumption. Indian teas continued in strong demand, with prices gradually tending upwards, stimulated by the improvement in quality.

Imports ..	..	164,000,000 lbs.,	against 182,000,000 lbs.	in 1872
Deliveries..	..	131,000,000 ,,	,, 127,000,000 ,,	,,
Exports ..	..	34,000,000 ,,	,, 39,000,000 ,,	,,
Stock (31st ult.) ..		97,000,000 ,,	,, 98,000,000 ,,	,,

Circular, 8th January, 1874.

Market firm. Steady business. Prices fully maintained for all kinds, with occasionally slight advance in medium to fine black leaf Congous. Stock, 97 million lbs., against 98 million lbs. in 1872.

Circular, 5th February, 1874.

General election interfered with business. Deliveries had been large. Stock, 92 million lbs., against 105 million lbs. in 1873.

Circular, 5th March, 1874.

Great dulness had prevailed. Small orders from the country. Prices for common to medium grades of Congou $\frac{1}{2}$d. decline in last fortnight. Stock, 95 million lbs., against 101 million lbs. in 1873.

Circular, 1st April, 1874.

Greatest dulness had prevailed during the past week. Deliveries had been very small. Prices unchanged. Stock, 95 million lbs., against 101 million lbs. in 1873.

Circular, 7th May, 1874.

Extent of business very limited. Prices unchanged, except for inferior green teas, which were 1d. per lb. lower. Stock, 83 million lbs., against 96 million lbs. in 1873.

Circular, 4th June, 1874.

Very little business. Several thousand boxes of new season's Tayshan Congous met with very poor reception. Prices generally un-altered, but new season's Tayshan Congou and green lower. Stock, 72 million lbs., against 83 million lbs. in 1873.

Circular, 2nd July, 1874.

Market continued in a state of stagnation. Almost entire business confined to public auctions. Prices unaltered. Stock, 61 million lbs., against 72 million lbs. in 1873.

Circular, 6th August, 1874.

Dealers bought cautiously. Brown leaf teas considered inferior in quality. Prices of fine Monings firmer. New Kaisows had sold 1d. per lb. lower than first day's sales. Old black leaf, good common to medium, ½d. per lb. lower. Stock, 61 million lbs., against 68 million lbs. in 1873.

Circular, 3rd September, 1874.

Market had been steadier, with fair amount of business. Common Foochow grades were 1d. per lb. lower. Stock, 74 million lbs., against 73 million lbs. in 1873.

Circular, 1st October, 1874.

Good demand for most classes of Congou, and prices rather better for the medium to fine grades of Kaisow. Other kinds unaltered. Stock, 74 million lbs., against 73 million lbs. in 1873.

Circular, 5th November, 1874.

Market continued extremely quiet, notwithstanding large deliveries of last month. Prices of black leaf Congous ½d. per lb. lower. Moyune kinds and Teenkais 1d. to 2d. per lb. lower. Stock, 77 million lbs., against 84 million lbs. in 1873.

Circular, 3rd December, 1874.

Market generally had been extremely dull. Prices of common grades of Foochow Congous slightly easier. Fychow and Moyunes show average fall of about 2d. per lb.

Annual Report, 5th January, 1875.

Had been fewer fluctuations than usual. In earlier months the trade demand was active, accompanied by some speculation, but the market collapsed, and continued depressed till the new crop came in, thus showing how small is the influence of any temporary reduction in stock. Losses had been considerable, not only owing to a relatively higher range of cost as compared with the first crop, but also to the increased shipments of these classes later in the season. The excitement attending the Adulteration Act had subsided, but its effects, coupled with continuous forced sales of Canton and green teas, had further influenced prices in those descriptions. *The whole range of values had been altered*, and unless a corresponding reduction could be made in cost, the style and proportions of the trade must be entirely changed. The state of the American market increased the depression of green teas. The home consumption showed an increase of six million lbs., but the export had again fallen off two million lbs. *Indian tea was affecting more and more the* VALUE of all the higher-priced China sorts, fancy kinds included, and especially those from Foochow, and it being certain that the quantity will increase, its growing influence on the China trade cannot well be over estimated.

Imports .. .. .. 158,000,000 lbs., against 164,000,000 lbs. in 1873
Deliveries .. .. 137,000,000 „ „ 131,000,000 „ „
Exportation .. .. 32,000,000 „ „ 34,000,000 „ „
Stock (Dec. 31, 1874) 85,000,000 „ „ 97,000,000 „ „

Circular, 7th January, 1875.

Market had continued quiet until after holidays, when there was a good demand for both descriptions of Congou. Arrivals numerous. Prices maintained. Stock, 85 million lbs., against 97 million lbs. in 1874.

Circular, 4th February, 1875.

Little doing; market quiet; quantity offering large. Lower rates ruled at public auction. Prices of brown leaf Congou rather lower; other kinds unaltered. Stock, 101 million lbs., against 92 million lbs. in 1874.

Circular, 4th March, 1875.

Business quiet. Prices unchanged. Stock, 97 million lbs., against 95 million lbs. in 1874.

Circular, 1st April, 1875.

Business fair. Prices of Congou unaltered, but scented and green teas rather better at public sale. Stock, 97 million lbs., against 95 million lbs. in 1874.

Circular, 6th May, 1875.

Market had continued in a dull and inactive state, notwithstanding large deliveries. Prices unaltered. Stock, 82 million lbs., against 83 million lbs. in 1874.

Circular, 3rd June, 1875.

Business limited. Market extremely quiet. Prices for fair Congous rather easier. New Tayshans 1d. per lb. lower. Stock, 71 million lbs., against 72 million lbs. in 1874.

Circular, 1st July, 1875.

Pending arrival of new teas private contract market suspended, and prices nominal. Scented Capers declined 1d. per lb. Stock, 71 million lbs., against 72 million lbs. in 1874.

Circular, 5th August, 1875.

Slight improvement. Quantity offering far greater than dealers can buy. Prices ½d. per lb. lower for fair to medium grades of brown leaf. Stock, 71 million lbs., against 61 million lbs. in 1874.

Circular, 2nd September, 1875.

Rather better demand for medium to fine grades of Congou. Prices occasionally showed some slight improvement, but for all common to fair descriptions lower rates ruled. Stock, 85 million lbs., against 74 million lbs. in 1874.

Circular, 7th October, 1875.

Large business had been transacted, and prices improved slightly, but a relapse soon occurred, the arrivals being heavy, and the probabilities of a war with China being for a time averted. Stock, 86 million lbs., against 74 million lbs. in 1874.

Circular, 4th November, 1875.

Great dulness had prevailed, with business very limited. Arrivals had again been heavy. Prices for common to black leaf Congou fully ½d. per lb. lower. Common green teas and Foochow scented teas also lower. Stock, 87 million lbs., against 77 million lbs. in 1874.

Circular, 2nd December, 1875.

Almost a cessation of business, excepting public sales, which had been of small extent. The arrivals had been very heavy, the stock in the United Kingdom being 97 million lbs., against 80 million lbs. last year. Prices generally unaltered, but at public auction, grades of Congous occasionally sold at easier rates. Stock, 97 million lbs., against 80 million lbs. in 1874.

Annual Report, 4th January, 1876.

The feature was the steady and large increase in the home consumption, *chiefly, however, of Indian growths*. The *whole of the China crop* being on offer within a few months, *instead of being spread over the year, as formerly, must necessarily affect prices in this market*. The consumer, on the other hand, benefited by the altered and *hurried mode* of trade. During the last two months of the year a large business was transacted, at advancing prices, but shortly after, notwithstanding the rapid reduction in stock up to the 30th June, great indifference was shown on the part of the trade, and prices gradually receded. The dispute between the dealers and importers as to *greater dispatch in the delivery of tea assisted also to depress the market*. For all common grades there had been a generally declining market, and the early arrivals opened lower than had been seen for some years. Uncertainty about the Adulteration Act, combined with the unsettled state of the American market, caused lower rates to rule than had ever been known.

Imports ..	..	195,000,000 lbs., against	158,000,000 lbs. in 1874
Deliveries..	..	145,000,000 ,,	,, 137,000,000 ,,	,,
Exports ..	..	32,000,000 ,,	,, 32,000,000 ,,	,,
Stock (31st Dec.,'75)	103,000,000 ,,	,, 85,000,000 .,	,,

Circular, 6th January, 1876.

Arrivals heavy. Quantity offering large. Demand better. Common grades unaltered. Fair to medium black leaf rather firmer. Stock, 103 million lbs., against 85 million lbs. in 1874.

Circular, 3rd February, 1876.

Moderate enquiry. At public sale common grades of Congou sold rather easier. Stock, 101 million lbs., against 101 million lbs. in 1875.

Circular, 2nd March, 1876.

Demand continued limited. At public sales common grades of Congou sold at lower rates. Prices for siftings to common Foochow Congous ½d. per lb. dearer. Common to fair grades of scented Capers and Foochow Pekoes ½d. per lb. dearer. Stock, 101 million lbs., against 97 million lbs. in 1875.

Circular, 6th April, 1876.

Market had been extremely quiet, and business limited. Quantity brought to auction large. Prices for black leaf ½d. per lb. lower; price of both descriptions 1d. per lb. down. Souchongs and Tayshan Congou ½d. to 1d. per lb. down. Stock, 92 million lbs., against 93 million lbs. in 1875.

Circular, 4th May, 1876.

Dealers continued to restrict their purchases as much as possible. Deliveries to end of April nearly one million less than last year, owing to falling off in export. Prices for Congous generally unaltered. A few medium to good occasionally rather dearer. Stock, 83 million lbs., against 82 million lbs. in 1875.

Circular, 8th June, 1876.

Principal business public sales, where a general decline had been established in prices. Stock, 70 million lbs., against 71 million lbs. in 1875.

Circular, 6th July, 1876.

Market had dragged heavily on, with transactions quite on a retail scale, and prices lower for most kinds. Prices for all old imports lower. Stock, 57 million lbs., against 58 million lbs. in 1875.

Circular, 3rd August, 1876.

Again a dull and dragging market, with constant public sales. Black leaf Congou unaltered, but fair to medium brown leaf and Paklings ½d. to 1d. per lb. lower. Stock, 68 million lbs., against 71 million lbs. in 1875.

Circular, 7th September, 1876.

Had been an improved feeling, although business transacted was only limited. At public auctions common grades had again sold lower. Stock, 90 million lbs., against 85 million lbs. in 1875.

Circular, 5th October, 1876.

Little alteration in tone of the market. Prices unaltered, except for scented teas, which were 1d. to 2d. per lb. dearer for common to medium. Stock, 99 million lbs., against 86 million lbs. in 1875.

Circular, 2nd November, 1876.

No improvement in tone of the market, the dealers still holding back from purchasing. Public sales rather larger than of late, and lower rates had ruled for most grades of Congou. Stock, 103 million lbs., against 87 million lbs. in 1875.

Circular, 7th December, 1876.

Excepting for common Congou for delivery, the enquiry for all other kinds most limited. Prices of Congous unaltered, but green teas 1d. per lb. lower for medium to fair grades. Stock, 105 million lbs., against 97 million lbs. in 1875.

Annual Report, 2nd January, 1877.

Record of last year formed no exception to late unsatisfactory series of annual reports, so far as importers were concerned. Only redeeming feature, a further expansion of clearances, but even these not in same ratio of increase as in the preceding year, while the export had fallen off $3\frac{1}{4}$ millions. Market had been " dragging and difficult," and the prices obtainable, as a rule, scarcely exceeded " commissions," even at the highest point, and then only for a small portion of the first crop medium grades ; *while of late the losses on the common to fair kinds had been heavy and continuous.* This was due to the general state of trade in 1876, the inferiority of the crop, *the rapid shipments in excess of the supplies of* 1875, AND THE INEVITABLE RESULT OF ACCUMULATING A STOCK BEYOND THE POWER OF THE TRADE TO COMPASS. The result had been almost constant depression, the impossibility of making sales beyond the daily requirements of the dealers unless by *forcing off at public auction,* thus leading to lower and lower prices in most instances, *while in the face of all this, shipments had been going on in China at rates confessedly above those ruling at home.* The fear of DETERIORA-TION in quality. It was significantly remarked that the imports from India were steadily increasing in amount and improving in quality, which must every year more and more affect the higher grades of China growth. The average price of Indian tea had been fully maintained, the increase of $3\frac{1}{2}$ millions being accompanied by an equal increase in the consumption.

Imports	..	.. 186,000,000 lbs., against 195,000,000 lbs. in 1875
Deliveries	..	150,000,000 ,, ,, 145,000,000 ,, ,,
Exportation	..	29,000,000 ,, ,, 32,000,000 ,, ,,
Stock	..	.. 110,000,000 ,, ,, 103,000,000 ,, ,,

Circular, 4th January, 1877.

Market had been dull and depressed. Prices for common grades of black leaf Congous ½d. per lb. lower ; common scented Capers ½d. per lb. dearer.

Circular, 8th February, 1877.

Market in unsatisfactory state. Sales impossible at any fair rates, Prices for fair to common grades of Congou ½d. per lb. lower, but at auction prices in some cases showed a heavy decline. Souchongs and Oolongs ½d. to 1d. per lb. lower. Finest lines of green teas fully 1d. per lb. dearer. Stock, 108 million lbs., against 101 million lbs. in 1875.

Circular, 8th March, 1877.

Business almost entirely confined to public sales, without reserve, Prices generally ½d. to 1d. lower for common to fair grades ; green teas, fine gunpowders, and Hysons 2d. per lb. lower. Stock, 103 million lbs., against 101 million lbs. in 1876.

Circular, 3rd May, 1877.

Past month had been extremely dull and quiet, the bulk of the business being at public auction. Prices of common to fair grades of Congou irregular, and slightly lower ; scented teas and green teas ½d. to 1d. per lb. lower. Stock, 88 million lbs., against 83 million lbs. in 1876.

Circular, 7th June, 1877.

Market during May continued dull and inactive throughout. Public sales had been about the same in amount. Prices of commonest grade of Congou slightly better; new Tayshan Congous 2d. per lb. ; scented teas 1d. ; green teas 1d. and 2d. per lb. lower. Stock, 76 million lbs., against 70 million lbs. in 1876.

Circular, 5th July, 1877.

New season's black leaf Congous had arrived. Quality considered inferior. Dealers showed indifference in purchasing. After first day's sale, large quantity sold, without reserve, at irregular rates, showing a reduction varying from 2d. to 3d. per lb. No enquiry for teas of old import. Business confined to public auction. Stock, 65 million lbs., against 57 million lbs. in 1876.

Circular, 2nd August, 1877.

Market had been steady, with fair amount of business. Prices unaltered. Stock, 79 million lbs., against 68 million lbs. in 1876.

Circular, 6th September, 1877.

Rather better enquiry, but extent of business very limited. Prices unaltered, excepting lower rates for the commoner grades of Congou. Stock, 87 million lbs., against 90 million lbs. in 1876.

Circular, 4th October, 1877.

Market continued extremely dull. Prices at auction ruled irregularly, but generally in favour of buyers. Stock, 96 million lbs., against 99 million lbs. in 1876.

Circular, 8th November, 1877.

Market continued in same dull and depressed state. At auctions irregular and lower rates ruled. Scented teas 1d. per lb. lower. Stock, 107 million lbs., against 103 million lbs. in 1876.

Circular, 6th December, 1877.

Continued reports of short export from China, added to large deliveries, had at length imparted some confidence. Prices for common grades of Congou ½d. per lb. dearer. Stock, 111 million lbs., against 105 million lbs. in 1876.

Thompson's Report, 4th January, 1883.

Results of tea trade for year 1882 had been unsatisfactory to importers, while the dealers had been able to *buy at cheaper rates than ever known—in several instances below the cost of production.* It was thought that prices had reached their lowest in 1881, but the average for the past year had been 15 to 20 per cent. less. The general trade depression would account in a measure for this, but it had been aggravated by the early and hurried supplies from China adding to the heavy stock in the warehouses on the 31st May; and further, by the anticipation of an excessive increase in the supplies from India. The quality of the crop also, both from China and India, had been inferior from several districts; but as regards Indian, improvement in this respect was reported, while the quantity would be less than was expected. The growth of the Indian export from year to year, it was added, must continue to exercise a marked effect upon the value of all good and fine China teas, more especially as the consumption of the former was largely on the increase.

Thompson's Report, 4th January, 1884.

The year 1883 had not been a profitable one to the importer, although the losses had been less severe than the previous season. The favourable feature was the expansion of the trade, as shown by the improved deliveries. The cost in China was moderate, but supplies being hurried forward quicker than ever from both China and India, there was naturally a greater pressure to realise, and the auctions being very heavy, the grades in over supply were brought down to a low level, from which they have only lately slightly recovered. The Indian crop did not show the increase at one time expected, but the Ceylon teas were appreciated, on account of flavour as well as strength, and the consumption was largely on the increase, to the detriment of China.

SUMMARY.

FINAL CONCLUSIONS DRAWN FROM THE FOREGOING FACTS AND ARGUMENTS.

SO long as the metal money of the world could be increased by private individuals being allowed to carry silver to the mints to be coined, it is evident that a gradual rise in prices over a long period would result from an increase in the volume of the metallic money in circulation. As regards silver, this is no longer possible in Europe, and prices have not been influenced by that cause for a period long anterior to the demonetisation of silver by Germany. Neither have prices been influenced by a decrease in the volume of silver money in circulation, because, since the price of silver has been falling from the period of the establishment of the Latin Union, silver for manufacturing purposes could be got cheaper by buying the raw material.

Gold may be said to have been minted exclusively by the European Governments for a long time past, and the requirements of the public have been satisfied as they have made themselves felt. In neither case, therefore, can it be alleged that the metal currencies of Europe have been forcibly increased simply for purposes of profiting by the conversion of the metal into money, as was formerly done upon no small scale. Consequently, the movement of prices in either direction cannot for a

long time past have been due to hidden influences of
that kind, which in a more primitive period no doubt
were the cause of movements of prices both up and
down over long periods of time.   The assumption, therefore, that the fall in prices which has occurred is due to
an order of influence that has died out appears to be an
erroneous one.   Further proof of this is afforded by the
investigations of the economists to whose writings we
have referred, which prove that a rise or fall in prices
respectively has always preceded and never followed an
expansion of the active metallic currency on the one
hand and a contraction on the other.

What appears to be the cause of a rise or fall in
prices, and what some authorities have held to be these
causes, are in reality not causes, but effects.   Had the
gold required by the different countries been abstracted
from the active circulations of the European communities
during the period referred to, the market value of money
at the great European centres could not have failed to
be so influenced, that a rise in the rates of discount of
the great national European banks must infallibly have
been the result.   We have shown that the European
markets were not appreciably disturbed—that not only
was no gold withdrawn from the store of the Bank of
England, but that, on the contrary, some was added to
it.   This we take to be a clear demonstration that, even
if it can be shown that the commercial supply of gold,
apart from that engaged in the active currencies of the
world, was diminished for the time by the sum more or
less roughly held to have been absorbed by Germany,
Italy, and the United States for gold currency purposes,

the rise in the relative value of the commodity gold
exercised an influence only upon the market value of
the metal, which influence was almost, if not entirely,
neutralised by the simultaneous action of the other
prices, which we have referred to in detail in the letter
quoted from the *Economist*.

The value of gold is after all but a relative value.
It is very easy to jump to the conclusion that because a
large demand for a thing springs up, there must be a
rise in its price and a scarcity of it, owing to its absorption. But gold occupies a very different position from
other commodities in this respect, that what is absorbed
for currency purposes, in the first place, does not dis-
appear as if consumed—is not perishable, except upon
an infinitesimal scale, compared with other perishable
articles. It is not at all inconceivable that at least three-
quarters as much old jewellery and other manufactured
articles of gold are melted down every year and re-
manufactured as there are articles manufactured out of
the new gold from the mines. There is much miscon-
ception on such points as these, and much erroneous
deduction drawn from false premises. Again, while
gold actively circulating may change relatively to commodities, while commodities may be said to remain
stationary, the converse may also take place. If the
quantity of commodities increases, no effect upon prices
is caused, unless the increased supply comes to market,
or there is reason to believe it will come to market. As
it is the aggregate of the purchases, constituting demand
on the one side, that influences prices over short periods,
as we have shown, so it is the aggregate of commodities

offering for sale and constituting supply that determines them on the other. So also is it the slowly-changing aggregate of gold actively employed which has been coined and has entered the markets, there to remain as circulating purchasing power, that regulates the level of prices over long periods.

One important factor in this discussion is, that a large amount of gold, probably a good deal more than was required for the new gold currencies, was liberated from its work by the fall in prices during the period under review. Not only was gold liberated from its work by that fall, but the new economic contrivances were simultaneously displacing the metal.

The large increase in the production of commodities was followed, first of all, by a struggle between the middle-man and the consumer. The former tried his best to keep up prices in the interests of his clients, the producers. When silver broke away from the fictitious level at which it had long been supported, Eastern merchants saw the deluge was upon them, and their only means of salvation was to "bear" Eastern produce. This opened the flood-gates, and down went prices, head over heels, silver among them. Like a collapse in the markets for public securities, where prices have been run up to a fictitious level of value for the purpose of "getting the public in," the fall in many things was as exaggerated as the previous rise. But it must always be remembered, in such ebbs and flows of values, that they very frequently go to extremes. There is no doubt that large numbers of habitual speculators in Eastern produce were ruined by the fall in prices, and they have been permanently scared off the ground, owing, in the first place, to their means being exhausted, and secondly, owing to there being no longer the same opportunity of making money by speculating.

The curtain behind which Polonius worked his arts, to the prejudice of the general public, and for the benefit of the army of Poloniuses who fattened in West-end palaces, has been drawn aside, never again to be a screen for the nefarious practices which have given so many people an unfair start in the great terrestrial race. We arrive, therefore, at the final conclusion, that the fall of prices of which so much has been heard was not only not due to any scarcity in the supply of gold, *but was, on the contrary, actually the cause of the supply increasing,* the fall in prices being itself the direct cause of the metal being displaced from active circulation, and this to a large extent furnishing the means, aided by the hoards, by which the countries referred to were able so easily, and without any disturbance to the loan, discount, or gold markets of the world, to effect the change in their standards of value, which continue to be maintained, apparently with ease, without causing any sort of inconvenience to any other nations.

APPENDIX.

A POTENT CAUSE OF THE FALL IN THE PRICE OF TEA.

Imports	1872, about	17,000,000	lbs.	Indian	Tea	
,,	1883,	,,	54,000,000	,,	,,	,,
,,	1872,	,,	166,000,000	,,	China	,,
,,	1883,	,,	161,000,000	,,	,,	,,
Deliveries	1872,	,,	16,500,000	,,	Indian	,,
,,	1883,	,,	59,000,000	,,	,,	,,
,,	1872,	,,	111,000,000	,,	China	,,
,,	1883,	,,	111,500,000	,,	,,	,,

The superior quality of Indian tea has had the effect of gradually transferring the bulk of the demand for fine teas to Indian teas, to the detriment of China teas of the finer grades. There is consequently each season a large quantity of the latter left, which during the last few months of the season have to be sold in absence of demand, and, therefore, at prices several pence below the ordinary average quotations of fine grades. The lower quotations of this reduced scale then naturally press on the medium grades just below, and so the entire scale of the remaining China teas has undergone the shrinkage which has been witnessed since about 1880.

Indian teas, therefore, have not only had the entire benefit of the increased consumption, but are also gradually usurping the bulk of the demand for teas of fine quality.

Unless any important alteration in the taste of the public, which may be easily influenced by the frequently expressed opinions of medical men that the considerably greater quantity of tannin contained in Indian tea makes this injurious to health, takes place, fine China growths will eventually entirely depend upon the demand for Russia, and the lower grades only be shipped to this country.

YEAR.	WAREHOUSE RETURNS.			CUSTOMS RETURNS. (Board of Trade.)	
	China.	Indian.	Totals.	Totals (only).	
1872	165,817,090	17,264,000	183,081,000	185,000,000	
1873	144,709,000	17,984,000	162,693,000	162,304,000	
1874	141,274,000	17,591,000	158,865,000	161,603,000	
1875	175,466,000	25,597,000	201,063,000	198,277,000	
1876	159,958,000	28,829,000	188,787,000	185,698,000	
1877	153,735,000	31,444,000	185,179,000	186,230,000	
1878	164,076,000	35,919,000	199,995,000	205,461,000	
1879	148,658,000	37,518,000	185,176,000	184,510,000	Indian.
1880	160,187,000	46,377,000	206,564,000	206,972,000	45,531,000
1881	163,159,000	44,585,000	207,744,000	212,463,000	45,054,000
1882	160,630,000	53,812,000	214,442,000	211,080,000	53,928,000
1883	161,000,000	61,968,000	222,968,000	222,006,000	60,995,000

THE ALLEGED APPRECIATION IN THE VALUE OF GOLD, AND THE FALL IN THE PRICES OF COMMODITIES.

To the Editor of the *Economist* (May 19th, 1883).

SIR,—Mr. Goschen's letter to the *Times* of Monday, the 7th inst., on this subject, confirms the impression made in my mind when I read his address to the Bankers' Institute, that he did not feel quite sure of his ground. Among others, I was curious to see upon what data Mr Goschen was going to make out his case, because the moment I heard that he intended to attribute the fall in prices mainly to a rise in the value of gold, I thought he was jumping too hastily to conclusions. Mr. Goschen's arguments have been attacked from several sides, Mr. Moxon, in the *Economist* of Saturday, the 5th inst., assisting in demolishing a position which I venture to think was not sufficiently reconnoitred before the assault was given, and, indeed, in my humble opinion, was not so put in a state of defence from the commencement as to be capable of resisting attack.

Let me first take the rise in prices, and see whether this can be accounted for by other causes the influence of which is more easily traced and gauged. It is well known, in the first place, that there was an outburst of business after the Franco-Prussian War, and that prices rose to a high point, until the commercial crisis in the United States in 1873, which went all round the world, caused a general reaction. That reaction continued, with brief intervals of recovery, up to the declaration of war by Russia against Turkey in the spring of 1877. The Mincing Lane authorities tell us that with the political difficulties in that quarter the real downward movement in some of the markets may be said to have commenced, and business continued more or less unsettled until September, 1879, when the great speculative movement set in. This caused prices to run up wildly until about the end of November, when the reaction ensued, followed by heavy losses, with some failures. Previous to this period there had been two important agencies at work tending largely to increase production, which is one of the main, if not the chief, causes of the low range of prices which has ruled since. The first of these was the inflated prices ruling for some time, and the second the flow of capital into new productive enterprise. The increase in the number of joint-stock companies of all kinds has been very large of late years, thus unduly stimulating competition, and preparing for difficulties which favourable circumstances may postpone, but which sooner or later must be felt by the holders of the vast quantity of shares which have been created.

The success of the Suez Canal has kept the markets largely supplied by steamers, and business has, besides, been revolutionised by the telegraph. Information regarding the coming crops in all parts of the world now reaches the retail trader and the consumer by wire, instead of by letter, as formerly. What was done by the Post Office before this change is now done by the morning and evening papers. The prolonged speculative movements of former years have to a great extent disappeared in consequence. This sudden opening of the markets to all classes of buyers has naturally given rise to very keen competition to secure business, which now results in small profits and great risks to all concerned. The recent action of the Bank of England towards the bill-brokers seems to be the beginning of a general movement among the banks, arising out of these changes, to get back into their old and safer grooves as regards advances for short periods. Up to recently, credit liabilities and advances on warrants and bills of lading seem to have been too freely granted, thus encouraging over-trading, while the bad harvests, and their effect upon trade, have contributed subsequently to the general inactivity. Wholesale dealers no longer secure supplies in anticipation of future requirements, which has a marked effect in preventing fluctuations. Then there has been depression in freights, the improved means of transit from the places of production to the ports of shipment, and the fall in the value of silver, all contributing to lower prices.

The greater competition in business drives the consumer to the cheapest market for everything, and to seek every means of securing what he requires at the smallest cost. Co-operative stores have brought prices down in every department, and as it becomes the fashion to be less ostentatious in domestic affairs, the prices of many articles not necessaries, and the charge for a variety of services, must be reduced also. These are some of the more easily tangible causes of the fall in prices to their present low level; but there are others not so easily seen unless carefully searched for, and which have apparently escaped Mr. Goschen's attention. That the general level of prices is determined, up to a certain point, by the quantity of the circulating medium in active existence is well known, but it has been long since recognised that prices can be forced up from their real to a nominally higher level for a time by other agencies, chief among which is credit. In proportion as confidence is inspired in the credit giver, *pro tanto* will prices become inflated, until circumstances bring about a reaction. Now, all who watch the course of commercial affairs are aware that there has been for years previous to the demonetisation of silver by Germany a large increase in the banking and credit-giving facilities afforded by all countries. New companies have not only afforded increased facilities, but have themselves been busily engaged in propagating their own species, notably in France, with the results which we see in the prostration of financial business, especially at Paris, for eighteen months past, and from which that and other French centres are still suffering. Here, then, is a potent factor, which has been at work practically ever since the conclusion of the Franco-German War. These new companies at first were the direct means of raising prices, and since, by assisting in the creation of every form of productive enterprise, have stimulated the reaction, from which there is up to the present time no recovery.

Again, there is the increase of fixed capital, which always exercises so much influence on prices at every renewed outburst of creative energy. It is well known that commodities do not vary much in value, their utility remaining the same, unless a greater or less quantity of labour is expended on their production ; but a rise in the value of the labour without any variation in its quantity will cau,,e a fall in the exchangeable value of commodities *in proportion to the increase in the amount of the fixed capital which is employed.* The greater the amount of fixed capital, the greater the fall in prices. Of late years there has been a very large increase in the fixed capital laid down all over the world, the most notable instance being in the United States, which accounts for the tenacity with which that Government adheres to the high tariff, and which is one of the chief causes of the low prices in the English iron markets. The low prices in many other departments can be accounted for in part also by the large increase in the amount of fixed capital brought to bear upon production. Every fall of profits lowers the relative value of those commodities produced with capital of a durable nature. The use of machines in all kinds of production has enormously increased, and as competition is stimulated values must come down. Moreover, such fixed capital being unavailable, like floating capital, for transfer at will to other industries, it must be kept going, and is often kept going at a loss in the hope of a recovery in values. Production on this basis means, as long as it can be maintained, the fall of prices to the minimum.

Attention should be directed to the composition of the table of figures given by Mr. Goschen showing the fall in prices. All the commodities enumerated are those of general necessity. It was long since pointed out by Mr. Tooke " that an excess of quantity operates in depressing the prices of commodities generally, but of corn more especially, in a ratio much beyond the degree of that excess." This was little noticed until the publication of the report of the Agricultural Committee of 1821. In that report it is stated : " A fall in the price of a commodity not of general necessity brings the article within the reach of a greater number of individuals, whereas in the case of corn, the average quantity is sufficient for the supply of every individual : all beyond that causes a depression of the market for a great length of time."

I have very briefly enumerated some of the more important hidden causes which have caused a decline in prices. I will now endeavour to discover whether the extra gold requirements of Germany, the United States, Italy, Scandinavia, &c., have had anything at all directly to do with the fall in prices.

The best of all guides, perhaps, to a solution of whether or not the value of gold has appreciated is its value in labour. Adam Smith's criterion of value is labour. Have wages fallen? No; on the contrary, they have risen, notwithstanding the increased means of transit by which idle labour can be brought to where it is wanted. Mr. Hankey humorously suggested that as the salaries in the Bank of England had been raised to meet the rise in prices which followed the discovery of the Australian goldfields, it was only fair that as Mr. Goschen maintained more could be bought now with the sovereign they should be lowered again.

There is no doubt that prices did rise then owing partly to those discoveries, because a new volume of gold was added to the world's active store, and partly to prices being raised through the exercise of a large new purchasing power; but the removal of a large quantity in existence as a commodity from one part of the world to another cannot be said at all to provide a basis upon which to found a converse proposition.

If this be admitted, then the fall in prices cannot be attributed to a material extent to the movements of gold to the countries mentioned. Besides, the gold thrown into circulation has taken the place of the silver thrown out, and we should consequently only have arrived at the *status quo ante*. The gold that has been absorbed by the countries referred to was not abstracted from the active circulation, to any material extent, of any other country, but was purchased as it could be picked up here and there from the floating surplus supply of the world. The surplus supply of gold has been diminished and that of silver increased, the difference being that silver has fallen through being abstracted from the active circulation, while the gold which has replaced it was not.

There is another point to which we have seen no reference made, and which in our view is very material. The fall in prices is much more likely to be due in part to the depreciation of silver than to the appreciation of gold. The holders of large quantities of silver have realised the loss represented by the fall in the relative value of that metal, and their purchasing power for a time has been correspondingly diminished. As the development of the use of substitutes for the precious metals proceeds, so in proportion is the effect lessened of any fluctuation in the total amount of the metallic currency in active circulation.

It will be said perhaps that the less there is in circulation to be acted on the greater will be the effect; but, on the other hand, the more the precious metals are dispensed with altogether, the less will the increase or decrease in the supply affect prices. Except as token money, silver has to a large extent returned, it may be said, whence it came, to its original state of existence as a commodity. Its resence, ptherefore, in active circulation exercises a greatly diminished effect upon prices.

So long as gold and silver together were exchangeable for commodities on the basis of the fixed ratio which existed everywhere, except in England, up to the time of the closing of the foreign mints to the free coinage of silver, which followed Germany's demonetisation of that metal, any increase or decrease in the active circulation of either metal would tend to influence prices in either direction.

We entertain very little doubt that the facilities afforded by foreign mints for the free coinage of silver have been the means, for a very long time past, of quite uselessly adding to the silver currencies of continental nations, and, through that addition, of raising prices for the benefit of producers, and at the expense of consumers.

It will perhaps be said in reply, you cannot force more currency into circulation than is required for the exchange of a given quantity of commodities, and that is no doubt true of paper or trust money, having only a local currency; but you can continue to force the precious metals into active circulation until you have reached a point when two half-crowns come to be the quantity of silver given in exchange for an article, which but for that unnecessary forcing of silver into active circulation could have equally well been exchanged for two shillings and sixpence.

If the bi-metallists had their way, we might go on charging the currencies of the world with metallic money, until at last we should have to give ten of our shillings for an article which we now purchase with two.

If such a process as this was not being carried out up to the period of closing all the continental mints to the free coinage of silver, how do we account for the continuous rise in the prices of commodities up to that period, and their continuous decline ever since?

The circumstance does not attract sufficient attention, that there is no longer the same importance attached to the intrinsic value of the precious metals by the individuals of a nation. England has taken the lead in this matter in respect of silver. For intrinsic value is being substituted trust in respect of the lower order of coins, as it has been for a long time with the larger forms of money. A five-pound bank note is taken on trust. Now that the value of silver has fallen, our shillings and half-crowns are nearer to their real value than they were before. Before the fall in the value of silver they also were taken on trust. They bore the stamp of the Mint upon them, as the five-pound notes bore the promise to pay five pounds of the Bank of England.

But this trust only to a limited extent carries any value beyond the borders of the country in which such currency is issued. Trust-money is, however, always obtaining currency over a wide area. Bills of exchange and cheques, within their respective limits, are trust-money. They pass from hand to hand for value, but only where the stamp of worth which they carry on their face is known.

As regards, therefore, the precious metals being distributed among the nations of the earth according to the commercial status of each, the automatic movement of silver has been materially interfered with. As regards England, it was, as we well know, ousted from its position as a partial indicator of prices.

After a very long interval, some three-quarters of a century, in fact, the barriers arresting the further progress of that movement have been thrown down by the Franco-German War.

The free passage of silver through the mints having thus been stopped, as regards silver Ricardo's law becomes inoperative, and prices, so far as the fluctuating supply of gold is concerned, will, we may assume, be henceforth affected by the quantity of that metal only in active circulation.

With reference to the special point upon which Mr. Goschen lays so much stress, it may be remarked that before it can be shown that prices have been influenced by what is called an appreciation of gold, it must be proved that some of the gold circulating as money has been withdrawn from active circulation, and that the mass, so distributed as to keep prices at the nominal level at which they were before any change was made, has sufficiently diminished as to cause an appreciable change in the general level of prices.

Because gold was exported from other countries to Germany to enable her to set up a gold currency, it does not necessarily follow that gold coins were abstracted from the various gold currencies and melted into 20-mark pieces. The probabilities, indeed, are, as we have already said, quite the other way, since bar gold is much more easily dealt with, and the process of converting it into genuine coins would be less expensive.

There is always a large surplus stock of gold in various parts of the world ready to come to any given point if $\frac{1}{8}$ or even $\frac{1}{16}$ per cent. profit can be made out of the operation of sending it to the purchaser.

For instance, in 1876 the stock of gold at the Bank of England rose to £35,000,000 on the 20th September, a difference of £14,000,000 compared with the present amount. Where did that gold come from? Was it abstracted from the circulating currencies of other countries? When eagles come from the United States, napoleons from France, or marks from Germany, are they ever melted into bars, and thus taken out of circulation? They remain here a short time, and then return from whence they came.

Writing on this subject in 1847, Mr. Tooke remarked as follows :— " But beyond the stock which is requisite for this purpose (as merchandise in transit), and which must always include more or less of surplus to meet occasional extra demand, there must be a very considerable amount of the precious metals applicable and applied as the convenient mode of adjustment of international balances, being a commodity more generally in demand and less liable to fluctuations in its market value than any other. I will not venture, in the absence of any recognised grounds for computation, to hazard an estimate of the amount so required; but bearing in mind the immense extent of international transactions, and the vicissitudes of the seasons and other circumstances affecting the relative imports and exports of gold, raw materials and manufactures, besides the variations in the market value of national and private securities held interchangeably, the quantity of bullion required to be constantly available for this purpose must be very large. Apart from the stores in the various banks, it must be occasionally increased by coin which has become superfluous in the circulation."

Unless there had been a surplus of gold available apart from the quantity actively engaged for currency purposes, I am of opinion that Germany could not have established a gold currency at all. To have attempted to abstract a sufficient supply from existing active currencies would have been an altogether hopeless task. The metal has been bought from the surplus supplies as it could be conveniently obtained, thus giving rise to the erroneous assumption that there was a struggle for gold, and that there was not enough for the use of the world. The fact of Germany, the United States, and Italy having procured what they wanted showed conclusively that, so far as the requirements of those countries were concerned, the gold in existence was sufficient to supply their wants, and if any other country contemplates following their example, a still further surplus supply would no doubt be forthcoming. Regarding the export of money from a country, Ricardo says, "However great the scarcity of coin might be, the exportation of money would be limited by its increasing scarcity. Money is in such general demand, and, in the present state of civilisation, is so essential to commercial transactions, that it can never be exported to excess; even in a war such as the present, when our enemy endeavours to interdict all commerce with us, the value which the currency would bear from its increasing scarcity would prevent the exportation of it from being carried so far as to occasion a void in the circulation."

Lastly, Mr. Goschen takes a range of prices over so short a period as ten years, and apparently believes that the change in the value of gold has been so rapid as to account for the fall in prices. Dr. Adam Smith says, when referring to changes in prices over the same period of ten years, that it is too sudden to be ascribed to any change in the value of silver, which is always slow and gradual, and he adds: "The suddenness of the effect can be accounted for *only by a cause which can operate suddenly*, such as the accidental variations of the seasons." In writing on this subject Mr. Tooke says of the close of the seventeenth century: "It is indeed manifestly impossible to discover any cause for the remarkably low prices from 1685 to 1692 but that of a succession of favourable seasons, *acting upon a probably extended cultivation*." Lord King, in a pamphlet published in 1804, stated that the rapid emission of assignats, as a consequence of the French Revolution, must have driven a large quantity of silver out of circulation; yet that violent operation does not appear to have produced any perceptible effect on prices, or even on the value of silver in Europe.

Mr. Tooke considers this evidence of Lord King "quite decisive against the hypothesis of a considerable influence on the value of the metals, by the quantity disengaged from the circulation of this country. The amount of coin circulating in France immediately previous to the Revolution was computed at nearly one hundred millions. Put it at seventy-four millions, Peuchet's estimate, nearly the whole of it was banished from circulation between 1790 and 1794, the major portion coming to England. No distinctly perceptible increase of the bullion prices of commodities followed this addition to the currencies of Europe," the fact being, of course, that the extra quantity was not really added to the other countries' circulation.

It would appear, then, from the evidence here adduced, that Mr. Goschen has been too hasty in attributing the fall in prices during the last ten years to an appreciation in the value of gold, that the fall is not to any material extent attributable to such appreciation, but that it has been the result of other causes to which I have referred.

Arthur Crump.

The *incomes* which purchased tobacco, spirits and beer did not suffer so much by the effects of the fall in the value of silver and the value of land as those which purchased tea, coffee, and sugar.

Mr. GOSCHEN'S PRICES.

	1873.	1883.	1888.	CHANGE IN LAST 5 YEARS.
Sugar, brown Manila ..	16/6 cwt.	12/- cwt.	9/- cwt.	— 3/- cwt.
Good and fine West Indian	29/- ,,	20/- ,,	14/6 ,,	— 5/6 ,,
Tea, sound common Congou	-/11½ lb.	-/5 to -/5½ lb.	-/4½ lb.	— -/1 lb.
Coffee, mid. Plantation Ceylon	87/- cwt.	70/- cwt.	75/- cwt.	+ 5/- cwt.
Cocoa, Guayaquil	59/- to 60/- cwt.	59/- ,,	68/- ,,	+ 9/- ,,
Wheat	£2 16/- qr.	£2 -/6 qr.	£1 12/- qr.	— 8/- qr.
Rice, Rangoon	9/6 cwt.	7/- cwt.	6/9 cwt.	— -/3 cwt.
Pepper	-/7 lb.	-/5½ lb.	-/7 lb.	+ -/1½ lb.
Metals—Iron, Scotch Pig ..	£6 7/- ton	£2 9/- ton	£1 18/10 ton	— 10/2 ton
Lead, English	£21 10/- ,,	£13 15/- ,,	£14 15/- ,, *	+ £1 ,,
Copper	£91 ,,	£65 ,,	£80 ,,	+ £15 ,,
Tin, Foreign	£142 ,,	£93 ,	£126 ,,	+ £33 ,,
Wool—English Sheep .. (half hoggett, half wether)	2/3 lb.	-/10¾ lb.	-/10¼ to -/10½ lb.	— -/0½ lb.
Mohair	3/3 ,,	1/8½ ,,	1/0¾ lb.	— -/7¾ ,,
Australian .. .. . (average Victoria, washed)	2/- ,,	1/10 ,,	1/5 to 1/6 lb.	— -/6 ,,
Alpaca	2/9 ,,	1/3 ,,	-/10¾ lb.	— -/4¾ ,,
Cotton, mid. Upland.. ..	-/9 ,,	-/5½ ,,	-/5⅜ to -/5½ lb.	--
Fair Surat	-/6¼ ,,	-/4¼ ,,	-/4¾ lb.	+ -/0½ lb.
Cochineal	2/5 ,,	-/10 ,,	1/1 ,,	+ -/3 ,,
Indigo	7/3 to 7/6 lb.	6/6 to 6/10 lb.	5/6 to 5/9 lb.	— 1/- ,,
Hides, River Plate, heavy ..	-/8½ lb.	-/7¼ lb.	-/5½ lb.	— -/1¾ ,,
Salted, light	-/8½ ,,	-/6½ ,,	-/5⅛ to -/5¼ lb.	— -/1¼ ,,
Jute	£16 ton	£10 10/- to £11 ton	£12 ton	+ £1 ton
Nitrate of Soda	16/- to 16/6 cwt.	12/- cwt.	10/- cwt.	— 2/- cwt.
Saltpetre	£1 10/6 ,,	19/- ,,	17/- ,,	— 2/- ,,
Wallsend (coals)	£1 10/- ton	18/- ton	16/6 ton	— 1/6 ,,

* This recovery was in sympathy with the rise in Copper and Tin.

SUGAR has gradually fallen since the duties were abolished in 1874. Extended production of beet, and the lowness of freights, have tended chiefly to the depression, also the excessive imports of foreign refined.

TEA.—The increased use of Indian and Ceylon. Indisposition of the trade to hold stocks, as tea will not keep.

COCOA (GUAYAQUIL).—This particular growth is influenced by the extent of crop, which varies. The chief consuming country is Spain, but during the last few years the use has increased amongst the trade here, and supply has barely or at times not kept pace with requirements.

COFFEE fluctuates with the crops, especially of Brazil, and is subject to constant speculative fluctuations. Ceylon high (now 85s.), owing to leaf disease and diminished production.

WHEAT.—Foreign importations and low freights.

RICE varies with grain market, and the production of late years has been very large. Bad potato crops generally stimulate speculation. Visible supply large, especially for Siam.

PEPPER.—The high prices caused by speculation entirely. Production " cornered."

SCOTCH PIG IRON.—Over-production, diminished requirements of America.

LEAD.—Extended production in Europe, also in America, greatly depressed prices. In Australia, a great deal produced. Both the latter contains much silver. The higher prices of other metals.

COPPER.—Influenced by the movements of the syndicate. Prices artificial. There is so much produced in America that prices must ultimately return to a moderate level. Visible supplies in England and France large.

TIN.—Entirely speculative, and much above former level, to which it may return.

COTTON took many years to fall from the " famine " prices ruling during the American War. Good crops American, low freights, have brought prices down to about their nominal position. Surat follows American.

COCHINEAL.—Present recovery owing to small stock here. Decreased consumption in this country, partly through the use of other dyes and the colour from cochineal going out of fashion.

INDIGO.—Supply rather in excess of demand. Less consumption of blue cloth, &c.

JUTE.—Prosperity of trade in Dundee.

NITRATE OF SODA.—Vastly increased production and break up of the combination in American markets. Depression in agriculture.

SALTPETRE.—Decreased consumption, nitrate of soda being largely used in the manufacture of gunpowder.